Alec + Kathy
Firth, 1978

Holy Spirit

By the same author and published by SPCK

Canterbury Pilgrim
The Christian Priest Today

Holy Spirit

A BIBLICAL STUDY

Michael Ramsey

LONDON
SPCK

First published 1977
SPCK
Holy Trinity Church
Marylebone Road
London NW1 4DU

Printed in Great Britain by
Richard Clay (The Chaucer Press) Ltd,
Bungay, Suffolk

ISBN 0 281 03586 5

Contents

Acknowledgements 6

Preface 7

1 Holy Spirit 9

2 The Spirit in the Mission of Jesus 19

3 St Luke: Nazareth, Jerusalem, Rome 33

4 The Witness of St Paul 45

5 St Paul: The Spirit and the Christian Life 57

6 Spirit, Fellowship, Church 74

7 St John: Spirit and Glory 89

8 St John: The Paraclete 100

9 Some Other Writers 111

10 Afterthoughts 117

Notes 132

Index of Biblical References 137

Acknowledgements

Thanks are due to the following for permission to quote from copyright sources:

A. & C. Black Ltd: *Spirit of God* (Bible Key Words) by E. Schweizer.

Basil Blackwell, Publisher: *The Gospel of John* by R. Bultmann.

Macmillan, London and Basingstoke: *The Holy Spirit in the New Testament* by H. B. Swete.

The Society for Promoting Christian Knowledge: *The Holy Spirit and the Gospel Tradition* by C. K. Barrett.

Quotations from the Revised Standard Version of the Bible, copyrighted 1946 and 1952 by the Division of Christian Education of the National Council of the Churches of Christ in the USA, are used by permission.

Preface

It is the purpose of this book to examine the experience which the Christians of the first century ascribed to the Holy Spirit, and the theology with which that experience was linked. The study discloses much variety of thought and language, but an underlying unity is apparent, inasmuch as the Spirit is constantly believed to be the Spirit of Jesus who died and rose again. I hope that the readers of this book will be helped in the study of its theme, which requires both awareness of the critical questions which are involved and sensitivity to the spiritual issues, for the theme is indeed on the borderline of theology and spirituality.

The doctrine of the Holy Spirit has returned to prominence at the present time both in Christian life and in theological study. There are the many forms of 'charismatic' revival, the problems of the relation between the Spirit's work in the Church and in the world, the questions concerning the Spirit and the theology of the triune God. There is also a contemporary tendency to separate Christian spirituality from the historical Jesus Christ. I hope that this book may assist in the study of these questions in the light of the experience and theology of the early Church.

The Revised Standard Version of the Bible has been used. Most of the biblical passages which are important for our study are not only cited but printed in full, so as to help the reader both to notice and to *meditate* upon the words of the New Testament writers, to 'chew and masticate them', as St Bernard somewhere says. It is by the response of imagination and will as well as the mind that we begin to grasp what the Spirit may do for us in taking 'what is mine' (John 16.14) and declaring it to us.

My thanks are due to Mr Douglas Dales of Christ Church College, Oxford, who undertook the laborious task of verifying biblical references throughout the book, and to Mrs Spiess at Cuddesdon who patiently typed the whole work from my manuscript.

Some of the material in this book was used in four lectures in Pastoral Theology given in the University of Durham in the Lent Term of 1976, and much of the material came into a course on the Holy Spirit and the Christian life given in the autumn of 1975 at Nashotah House, Wisconsin, on the first of a series of teaching visits to that seminary. For the happiness, friendship, and stimulus of those visits, my wife and I are deeply grateful. Before this book appears, it will have been my privilege to deal with some other aspects of the Spirit in the 1977 centenary lectures at Trinity College, Melbourne.

Durham ✠ MICHAEL RAMSEY
June 1977

1
Holy Spirit

The words 'Holy Spirit' describe a large part of Christianity. It has always been the belief of Christians that God revealed himself in a unique way in the story of Jesus, and this belief has given to Christianity its character as an historical religion. But Christians also believe that this revelation is corroborated in experience through a divine power in saintly lives in the subsequent centuries. It is this experiential, inward aspect of Christianity which is the theme of this book.

Here indeed is a vast and exciting field for the student of Christianity. A host of questions arise. What are the characteristic marks of the influence of Holy Spirit upon human lives? How is the power of Holy Spirit within the Christian community related to divine activity within the world as a whole? How may claims concerning the Spirit presence be tested? What is the link between the historical events of the Gospel and Christian spirituality in successive centuries? There are also the deep theological questions concerning Holy Spirit and the being of God. It is hoped that the chapters which follow may help in the understanding of these questions.

The method will be to discuss what Holy Spirit meant in the experience, the thought, and the language of the early Christians; and the book is therefore primarily an historical and biblical study in which we explore the evidence of the New Testament writers. If we cannot enter wholly into their thought and experience we can yet be sure that there are none from whom we can learn more about a theme so intimately linked with the coming of Jesus Christ.

The apostles saw both the coming of the Christ and the experience of Holy Spirit as the climax of a preparation in the Old Testament, and Hebrew thought-forms had their part in the early Christian concepts. Here then will be our starting-point, though we shall soon be considering also thought-forms of the Graeco-Roman environment of early Christianity. Nothing was, or is, more characteristic of Holy Spirit than the power to use and transform people, thought, and language.

Behind the meaning of the Holy Spirit for Christianity there lie concepts in the Old Testament which form the background for the mission of our Lord and the teaching of the apostles.

'Spirit' in the writings of the Old Testament is not a person or a definable object or substance. It is a mode of describing how the holy God is active in the world which he created, and especially in persons in whom his purpose is fulfilled.[1]

There are two Hebrew words which appear as 'spirit' in English versions of the Bible. One of the words is *nephesh*, which means 'breath'. It is in virtue of having breath within him that a man is alive, for the breath animates the physical organs. Thus when Elijah prays for the restoration of the dead child of the widow at Zarephath 'the child's *nephesh* returned upon his inward parts and he lived' (1 Kings 17.22). By a process of refinement *nephesh* came also to be used of the inner consciousness (Exod. 23.9) or the emotional life (Job 20.3); and in post-exilic times it is no longer specially associated with physical energy, for it now denotes what we might call the 'spirit' of a man, in the sense of his 'character' (Zech. 12.1).

The other word, more significant for theology, is *ruach*, or wind. It is by God's wind that the world and mankind are created and nature is continually sustained. No writing depicts this better than Psalm 104, where all living creatures, including man, are described as depending upon God's ceaseless energy:

> When thou hidest thy face, they are dismayed; when thou takest away their breath, they die and return to their dust. When thou sendest forth thy Spirit, they are created; and thou renewest the face of the ground (Ps. 104.29–30).

There could scarcely be a more vivid account of the dependence of the world upon the constant sustaining action of a creator who is both beyond the world and deeply active within it.

The creator's activity in the world extends not only to the continuing existence of his creatures but to their character in relation to God's purpose. Do men sometimes have remarkable powers, gifts, or aptitudes? These are the work of divine *ruach*, 'invading' men and women. To *ruach* are ascribed the physical strength of a Samson (Judg. 14.6), the leadership of a Joshua (Num. 12.18), the wisdom of sages (Prov. 1.23), the ecstasy of the sons of the prophets (1 Sam. 10.10). In this way *ruach* is not merely producing a series of outstanding human specimens, but is serving God's righteous purpose for mankind. So, not surprisingly, *ruach* is specially apparent in the inspiration of prophecy. It is by *ruach* that the prophets prophesy, and the implication is that Spirit inspires not only the ecstasy which they sometimes experience but the *mes-*

sage of which they are conscious and the impulse to deliver it. 'As for me,' says Micah, 'I am filled with power, with the Spirit of the Lord, and with justice and might, to declare to Jacob his transgression and to Israel his sin' (Mic. 3.8). The Lord's servant is described in Second Isaiah as being endowed with *ruach* for his mission to Israel and beyond Israel to the nations (Isa. 42.1).

Not surprisingly, Spirit comes to be used in the prophecies of the future fulfilment of God's purpose. As the words 'glory' and 'kingdom' tell both of present realities and of a future hope, so too the word 'Spirit' comes into the picture of the good things to come. There will be a day of deliverance, and when it arrives Spirit will be manifested in new ways: in a Messiah, in a people, and in the cosmos.

It is notoriously difficult to be sure either of the historical context or of the precise future reference of some of the prophecies about the future 'messianic' age. So let it suffice to assemble some of the passages which tell of the future action of Spirit within the scene of a glorious future.

In the Book of Ezekiel, who prophesies in the time of the exile of the Jews in Babylon, there are predictions of the future restoration of the community of Israel. Invaded himself by divine *ruach*, Ezekiel foretold that *ruach* would cause a moral revolution in the people:

I will give them one heart, and put a new spirit within them; I will take the stony heart out of their flesh and give them a heart of flesh, that they may walk in my statutes and ordinances and obey them; and they shall be my people, and I will be their God (Ezek. 11.19–20).

In another passage, words are used which later found their way into the Christian rites of initiation:

I will take you from the nations, and gather you from all the countries, and bring you into your own land. I will sprinkle clean water upon you, and you shall be cleansed from all your uncleannesses, and from all your idols I will cleanse you. A new heart I will give you, and a new spirit I will put within you; and I will take out of your flesh the heart of stone and give you a heart of flesh. And I will put my spirit within you, and cause you to walk in my statutes and be careful to observe my ordinances (Ezek. 36.24–7).

More dramatic is the prophecy of the valley of dry bones, a parable of the nation's restoration from the death of exile to the life of its true role in history.

Prophesy to these bones, and say to them, O dry bones, hear the word of the Lord. Thus says the Lord God to these bones: Behold, I will cause breath to enter you, and you shall live. And I will lay sinews upon you, and will cause flesh to come upon you, and cover you with skin, and put breath in you, and you shall live; and you shall know that I am the Lord (Ezek. 37.4–6).

Invoking the Spirit upon the dry bones in the valley, the prophet witnesses the Spirit coming to them from the four winds of heaven until they come alive and stand upon their feet, 'an exceedingly great host' (Ezek. 37.10). Here is the imagery of the resurrection of a nation from exile and despair into new life in God's purpose.

In the Book of Isaiah there is the picture of the messianic king endowed by the Holy Spirit for his office:

There shall come forth a shoot from the stump of Jesse, and a branch shall grow out of his roots. And the Spirit of the Lord shall rest upon him, the spirit of wisdom and understanding, the spirit of counsel and might, the spirit of knowledge and the fear of the Lord (Isa. 11.1–3).

And in the latter part of the book, of post-exilic date, there is the description of a spirit-filled messenger of God in words which our Lord is described by St Luke as quoting in the synagogue at Nazareth:

The Spirit of the Lord God is upon me, because the Lord has anointed me to bring good tidings to the afflicted; he has sent me to bind up the broken-hearted, to proclaim liberty to the captives, and the opening of the prison to those who are bound; to proclaim the year of the Lord's favor, and the day of vengeance for our God (Isa. 61.1–2).

Finally, we notice the passage in the Book of Joel, which the writer of Acts describes St Peter quoting on the day of Pentecost:

And it shall come to pass afterward, that I will pour out my spirit on all flesh; your sons and your daughters shall prophesy, your old men shall dream dreams, and your young men shall see visions. Even upon the menservants and the maidservants in those days, I will pour out my spirit (Joel 2.28–9).

Spirit will invade the entire community with portentous signs to show.

In all these ways we see that Spirit is a part of the Hebrew theology, with the prevailing imagery of wind. Spirit is not a thing-in-itself, or a person-in-himself, or a philosophical entity in itself; it means that God himself is active in the world. He is a God at once beyond and within, the creator and sustainer of his creation, manifesting himself in particular events and persons to forward his righteous purpose, and preparing the way for its future climax. Christians believe that this climax is Jesus of Nazareth.

Besides the language and thought of the Hebrew Old Testament, we need to take into account the language and thought of later Judaism, of the Greek-speaking Judaism in Alexandria which produced the Book of Wisdom, and of the pagan world in which the Greek word *pneuma* could be used in ways both akin to and very different from the Hebrew *ruach*.

In later Judaism the main concepts about Spirit familiar in the Old Testament writings continue, but with the formation of the Canon of Scripture there came the tendency to look back to the days when the Spirit spoke through the prophets and to dwell upon the inspiration by which the sacred books had been written. There was an increasing emphasis upon the conscious possession of a tradition of sacred history, law, and prophecy, a tradition in which Spirit had been at work revealing the character and will of God. At the same time there was a looking forward, beyond the frustrations of the present time, to the coming of the Messiah, and a literature appeared which foretold a Messiah in the manner of the Isaiah prophecies, sometimes with an apocalyptic and sometimes with a more political emphasis. Thus the *Psalms of Solomon*, a work written in Pharisaic circles about 50 B.C., contained a beautiful prophecy of a messianic king: 'The Lord made him mighty in the Holy Spirit' (*Ps. Sol.* 17.37). And the same theme appears in the *Testament of the Twelve Patriarchs*, probably written earlier (*Test. Levi.* 18.7). The latter work contained a picture of the moral renewal of hearts and minds by 'the spirit of salvation' and 'the spirit of grace'.

So far our account has been within the mainstream of Hebrew theology; but the rabbis sometimes moved into new speculative concepts. One development is the ascription to Spirit of actions of a personal kind: the Spirit is described as speaking, warning, grieving, weeping, rejoicing, consoling.[2] Yet this use of personal language did not imply that Spirit was thought of as an angelic being; rather did it suggest an emphasis upon the personal character of God's encounters. Another development is a kind of dualistic use of 'Spirit', as men face a conflict between a 'spirit of light' and a 'spirit of darkness'. This use is found in the Dead Sea Scrolls, within the work called the *Manual of Discipline* (cf. 3.20–5). But in these texts the power of God is presented as ultimately prevailing, and no permanent dualism disturbs the traditional monotheism. Yet another development is an increase in the use of 'Spirit' as meaning a person's own self or character.[3] These developments provide some of the background of thought and language to the New Testament writings without introducing any really new theological principle.

Among the Greek-speaking Jews of the dispersion, whose Bible was the Greek version called the Septuagint, a more distinctive development is seen. In the Alexandrine work *The Wisdom of Solomon*, written probably in the first half of the first century B.C., the concept appears of Wisdom as the divine agent in creating and sustaining the world and illuminating the human race. Already known in the Palestinian Book of Proverbs in a poetic form (cf. Prov. 8 especially), this concept is here used in a more philosophical form and is identified with the Spirit of God (*pneuma*):

> The Spirit of the Lord has filled the world, and that which holds all things together knows what is said (*Wisd.* 1.7).

In chapters 6 and 7 are beautiful descriptions of Wisdom's relation to mankind, to be loved and cherished as the source of faith and goodness. She penetrates all things, and renews all things, and

> in every generation she passes into holy souls and makes them friends of God and prophets (*Wisd.* 7.27).

That Greek as well as Hebrew concepts are in the writer's mind is seen from his belief in the immortality of the soul (cf. *Wisd.* 3), and from a certain affinity between his doctrine of cosmic wisdom and the Stoics' indwelling *Logos*. There is a clear resemblance between the concept of Wisdom in this work and the concept of the *Logos* in the prologue of the Gospel of St John; the divine word who creates the world gives life to all created things and light to mankind. We shall find that the New Testament writers do not use the word *spirit* with this cosmic reference, for their thought about Spirit is intensely concentrated upon Christ and upon the Church as the eschatological community. But St John's doctrine of *Logos* witnesses to the cosmic activity of the creator.

Just because the Hebrew word *ruach* had *pneuma* as its Greek equivalent, a body of Greek ideas and associations were part of the background of early Christianity. Our method in this book is to deal with these questions as and when they arise; and we shall see how both St Paul and St John make use of Greek concepts in their exposition of the gospel of Jesus Christ, but in such a way as to witness to the Hebrew monotheism and the messianic history from which Christianity sprang.

2
The Spirit in the Mission of Jesus

The Synoptic Gospels were written within the Christian Church after several decades of the Church's preaching, teaching, and worship. It was a preaching, teaching, and worship in which, as we shall see, the experience of the Holy Spirit and the doctrine of the Holy Spirit were very prominent. It is therefore the more striking that in the record of the teaching of Jesus in the Synoptic Gospels there is very little reference to the Holy Spirit; and this fact is indeed evidence that the gospels retain much of the early pre-crucifixion perspective. St Luke is a partial exception, for Holy Spirit is one of his favourite themes; but even he, while he emphasizes the Spirit as the power by which Jesus fulfilled his ministry, introduces only a few references to the Spirit in his record of the sayings of Jesus.

There is, however, within the synoptic tradition, a variety of linguistic usage, which reflects the ways of thinking of the Holy Spirit within the apostolic age. On the one hand, Spirit is sometimes described in the manner of the Hebrew *ruach* as a power, like wind or fire, which invades a person from without. On the other hand, there are descriptions of Spirit as a fluid or substance within a person, so that the person can be 'filled' with Spirit. In the one case, the person acts 'spiritually' under the impact of a kind of invasion. In the other case, the person acts 'spiritually' in virtue of something within him, a continuing possession which he himself may be able to pass on to others. In an analysis of the variety of language, R. Bultmann described the former usage as 'dynamic' and the latter as 'animistic', and he shows how the two interpenetrate in the New Testament writings. Refusing to see here an antithesis between Hebrew and Hellenistic concepts, he wrote: 'Neither conception is foreign to the Old Testament.'[1]

We find this contrast appearing in the Synoptic Gospels, when Mark writes that after the baptism of Jesus the Spirit 'drove' him out into the wilderness to be baptized (Mark 1.12); whereas Luke writes: 'Jesus, full of the Holy Spirit, returned from the Jordan, and was led by the Spirit for forty days in the wilderness' (Luke 4.1).

Luke indeed presents Jesus as one whose life is perpetually guided by the Spirit, one who is full of the Spirit, and one who is indeed himself Lord of the Spirit, able himself to bestow Spirit – as was to happen on the day of Pentecost. It would seem a mistake to regard St Luke's usage as Hellenistic. Rather may his language suggest that with the coming of Jesus the age of fulfilment is here. Spirit fills the Messiah, and the Messiah is to be God's agent in the pouring of Spirit upon those who believe.

THE BAPTIST AND THE BAPTISM OF JESUS

The beginning of the gospel, as Mark presents it, is the appearance of John in the wilderness of Judaea, 'preaching a baptism of repentance for the forgiveness of sins' (Mark 1.4). Many people came to the Jordan, and were baptized, confessing their sins.

The non-Marcan tradition spells out the preaching

of John more fully. Its keynote is the divine judgement upon the nation, and the need to repent because judgement is imminent.

> You brood of vipers! Who warned you to flee from the wrath to come? Bear fruit that befits repentance, and do not presume to say to yourselves, 'We have Abraham as our father'; for I tell you, God is able from these stones to raise up children to Abraham. Even now the axe is laid to the root of the trees; every tree therefore that does not bear good fruit is cut down and thrown into the fire (Matt. 3.7–10; cf. Luke 3.7–9).

With judgement near, membership in the chosen people gives no security; and as baptism was a rite normally associated with the reception of proselytes, it was a radical revolution to call upon the chosen race themselves to be baptized – an urgent cleansing before the divine blow falls.

Besides his message for the present, John has a prophecy for the future. A greater one is coming:

> After me comes he who is mightier than I, the thong of whose sandals I am not worthy to stoop down and untie (Mark 1.7).

In contrast with John's own baptism in water, the one who is mightier will have another baptism to bring. What will this other baptism be? In Mark's text it will be a baptism *with the Holy Spirit*. In the non-Marcan texts it will be a baptism *with the Holy Spirit and with fire*. And the non-Marcan texts emphasize the fire very strongly:

> He will baptize you with the Holy Spirit and with fire. His winnowing fork is in his hand, and he will

clear his threshing floor and gather his wheat into the granary, but the chaff he will burn with unquenchable fire (Matt. 3.11–12; cf. Luke 3.16–17).

If Mark's account gives us the true version, then there is a straightforward contrast between John's baptism in water and the subsequent baptism given by Jesus which involved the bestowing of the Holy Spirit. There is no evidence that Jesus himself administered a rite of baptism, but the baptism conducted by the apostles from the day of Pentecost onwards was a rite with water connected with the gift of the Holy Spirit – a gift which Jesus, risen and exalted, had 'poured forth' (Acts 2.33). If, however, the non-Marcan tradition is to be preferred, there is a question into which we must probe further.

It might be that the words 'Spirit' and 'fire' were seen in the Church's tradition as a forecast of Pentecost, a theme which would appeal to Luke. It might be that the original form of the tradition was in reference to *two* future baptisms – a baptism of Spirit to those who received the gospel, and of fiery judgement to those who rejected it. It might be that the prediction was solely one of the divine judgement which the mightier one would bring. The words which follow dwell upon judgement with sharp emphasis; but it is the judgement of sifting of wheat and chaff. It is well to remember that the blessings of the gospel and the sword of judgement go together. The child Jesus was set for the rise and the fall of many (Luke 2.34).

It is interesting to glance at the poignant saying of Jesus in Luke 12.49–50:

I came to cast fire upon the earth; and would that it were already kindled! I have a baptism to be baptized with; and how I am constrained until it is accomplished!

The mission of Jesus is to bring judgement into the world, and he longs for its fulfilment, since with it God's purposes are bound up. He has himself to be plunged beneath waters of calamity and suffering; and until this happens his mission is constricted.

In the course of the mission of the Baptist, Jesus himself comes to the Jordan and is baptized by John. What exactly happened? Christian art depicts Jesus standing in the water and John pouring water over his head; but it is more likely that Jesus, like all the others who were baptized, dipped himself into the water (cf. Luke 3.21, where the 'middle voice' of the verb is used both of the people and of Jesus). The reason for his baptism need not be pursued here; Jesus was fulfilling all righteousness (Matt. 3.15) in identifying himself with the people's response to John's call to the nation. He was 'made like his brethren in every respect' (Heb. 2.17). Our present study is concerned with an event which happened at the time, the descent of the Holy Spirit upon Jesus and the voice proclaiming his Sonship:

> In those days Jesus came from Nazareth of Galilee and was baptized by John in the Jordan. And when he came up out of the water, immediately he saw the heavens opened and the Spirit descending upon him like a dove; and a voice came from heaven, 'Thou art my beloved Son; with thee I am well pleased' (Mark 1.9–11).

Each of the synoptists prefixes this episode to the ministry of Jesus and attaches great importance to it.

If Mark describes what could be an experience observed by Jesus alone, Matthew and Luke 'objectify' the incident. In Matthew the voice is not addressed to Jesus alone, but it proclaims Jesus: '*This* is my beloved son.' In Luke the dove is described as being 'in bodily form'. As told in the early Church, the story would teach that Jesus is Son and Servant, recalling Psalm 2.7, 'You are my son,' and Isaiah 42.1, 'Behold my servant, whom I uphold.' It would teach also that at this same moment Holy Spirit was given to Jesus for the fulfilment of his mission. Such teaching is seen in the speech ascribed to Peter at Caesarea (Acts 10.37–8).

Why the sign of the dove? There was a tradition among the rabbis that the Spirit is like a dove, drawing upon the imagery of Genesis 1.2 where in the creation of the world the Spirit brooded like a bird over the face of the water. Collecting a number of instances of this idea from the rabbinic writings and the Targums, C. K. Barrett summed up thus:

> We cannot hold that the precise meaning of the dove symbolism has been certainly determined. But it is very important that the evidence, such as it is, points to the text which we found fundamental in our discussion of the birth narratives, to Genesis 1.2; that is to say that here too we have to deal with the creative activity of the Spirit. A new thing was being wrought (at the baptism) comparable with the creation of heaven and earth out of primaeval chaos.[2]

With the mission of the Messiah, as with his birth, a new order, a new creation, is on its way.

Thus at the time of his baptism Jesus is empowered by the Holy Spirit for his ministry as Son and Servant. In the Church's subsequent theology the episode was seen as the prototype of the Church's rite of baptism, the gift of the Spirit being linked with the immersion in water. In the event itself it would seem that Jesus' identification of himself with the baptism of John was one happening and his receiving of the Holy Spirit for his mission was another, there being no causal or sacramental link between the two (St Luke's account in particular suggests this; see Luke 3.21–2). By the words which were heard and by the gift which he received, Jesus was designated for his mission and empowered to fulfil it. 'It is the interaction of sonship and Spirit that gives Jesus' ministry its distinctive character.'[3]

THE MINISTRY OF JESUS

The first act of Jesus after the receiving of the Holy Spirit beside the river Jordan was to go to the wilderness to be tempted by the devil. Mark records that Jesus was tempted. Matthew and Luke describe the three specific conflicts with the tempter. If the temptation was in one sense the making of preliminary decisions about the course of the ministry, in another sense it was an integral part of that ministry. There is evidence that Jesus understood his mission as a conflict with supernatural evil, for he speaks thus to the Pharisees at the time of the Beelzebul controversy (Matt. 12.22–9; Luke 10.14–22).

Each of the synoptists describes Jesus as performing a ministry of teaching, healing, exorcism, and mighty works. It is by a more than earthly power that the ministry proceeds; and several words are used to describe this: authority (*exousia*), power (*dunamis*), and spirit (*pneuma*). The first two words are characteristic of all the synoptists, the third, specially of Luke, in descriptions of Jesus' ministry.

Jesus taught with authority (Mark 1.22).

Jesus rebukes unclean spirits with authority (Mark 1.27).

Jesus has authority to forgive sins (Mark 2.10).

Jesus has authority to drive out demons (Mark 3.15).

Jesus felt that power to heal had gone out from him (Mark 5.30).

The power of the Lord was present to heal (Luke 5.17).

If the powers had been wrought in Tyre and Sidon, they would have repented (Luke 10.13).

Stay in the city until you receive power (Luke 24.49).

Luke's interest in the Spirit is seen:

Jesus, full of the Holy Spirit, returns from the Jordan (Luke 4.1).

Jesus returns to Nazareth in the power of the Spirit (Luke 4.14).

The Spirit of the Lord is upon me (Luke 4.18).

Jesus rejoiced in the Holy Spirit (Luke 10.21).

It is in the nature of the authority, the power, and the Spirit that the character of the mission of Jesus lies.

'Power' and 'Spirit' had characterized the prophets in the past, so for Jesus to act by power and Spirit might involve no new principle in the history of God's people. 'Authority' hinted at more than this, for the authority of Jesus was such that he could put his own word from God against and above the ancient biblical tradition and radically reinterpret the law of Moses:

You have heard that it was said ... but I say to you ... (Matt. 5.27; 5.33; 5.43).

The authority of Jesus, and the power and Spirit by which he acts, are illuminated by these sayings which suggest that in his works, his teaching, and his presence, the day of fulfilment, the day of the new order, is here.

> Blessed are the eyes which see what you see! For I tell you that many prophets and kings desired to see what you see, and did not see it, and to hear what you hear, and did not hear it (Luke 10.23–4; cf. Matt. 13.16–17).

> Something greater than Solomon is here ... something greater than Jonah is here (Luke 11.31–2; cf. Matt. 12.6).

> If it is by the finger of God that I cast out demons, then the kingdom of God has come upon you (Luke 11.20; cf. Matt. 12.28).

The fulfilment is here, the time which the prophets had associated with the outpouring of Spirit. Yet there is still a frustration, a hiddenness, for the Christ must suffer and die. Only then will the era of the Spirit be openly proclaimed and the Spirit be bestowed on those who believe.

If the nature and context of Jesus' authority is seen in the sayings which hint that his ministry marks the time of fulfilment and the new era, so too is it seen in the sayings which tell of his sonship in relation to the Father, and his use of the word *Abba*.[4] This is a vast subject, and here we can note only its connection with the Holy Spirit. Why, it is asked, did Jesus not speak more about the Holy Spirit in connection with his own mission and authority? A partial answer may be that for Jesus the result of being filled with the Spirit was a heightening awareness of the Father whose work Jesus was doing. This is suggested in a striking passage of Luke:

> In that same hour he rejoiced in the Holy Spirit and said, 'I thank thee, Father, Lord of heaven and earth ...' (Luke 10.21).

The impulse of the Spirit evokes thanks and praise to the Father. Indeed 'it is the interaction of sonship and Spirit that gives Jesus' ministry its distinctive character'.[5]

THE SAYINGS OF JESUS

In the light of all this it is remarkable but also understandable that according to the synoptists Jesus said very little about the Spirit.

Of the few sayings about the Spirit in the synoptic tradition some appear to show the editorial hand of an evangelist. Thus there is the saying, 'If it is by the finger of God that I cast out demons...' and it is hard to doubt that Matthew's version, 'If it is by the Spirit of God that I cast out demons,' is due to editing and is less primitive (Luke 11.20; Matt. 12.28). Again, a saying about God's answer to prayer reads in Matthew 7.11: 'How much more will your Father who is in heaven give good things to those who ask him?' and in Luke 11.13 'good things' is replaced by 'the Holy Spirit'. Here too it is likely that 'Holy Spirit' comes from an editorial hand.

But there are two complex groups of passages referring to the Holy Spirit which call for special attention, as it is more likely that in them the mention of Holy Spirit belongs to primitive tradition. One is the

Beelzebul controversy, the other is the saying about what the disciples are to say when brought before rulers and magistrates.

1   The controversy about Beelzebul, with the saying about blasphemy against the Holy Spirit, occurs in both a Marcan and a non-Marcan form. The context is the allegation of the Pharisees that Jesus has been casting out devils by Beelzebul, the prince of the devils, and his reply that on the contrary he casts them out by the finger of God. In Mark's account the climax is the terrible saying:

> 'Truly, I say to you, all sins will be forgiven the sons of men, and whatever blasphemies they utter; but whoever blasphemes against the Holy Spirit never has forgiveness, but is guilty of an eternal sin' – for they had said, 'He has an unclean spirit' (Mark 3.28–30).

By his final comment Mark links the saying plainly with the preceding controversy. In the non-Marcan version Matthew has, in the same context:

> Therefore I tell you, every sin and blasphemy will be forgiven men, but the blasphemy against the Spirit will not be forgiven. *And whoever says a word against the Son of man will be forgiven; but whoever speaks against the Holy Spirit will not be forgiven, either in this age or in the age to come* (Matt. 12.31–2).

The words in italics come also in Luke, but in another context: the teaching about the reception given to the apostles when they bring their message (Luke 12.10).

It is not difficult to picture the historical situation

with some certainty. In their bitter hostility some of the Pharisees are attributing the beneficent works of Jesus to a power of evil, being content in effect to call good evil and white black. This is a kind of moral blindness which, if persisted in, finds no forgiveness, for it can lead on to a stifling of conscience and the sight of the truth may never come. It is on these lines that Christian preachers and pastors through the centuries have interpreted the blasphemy against the Spirit. And when scrupulous people torment themselves about whether they have committed the unforgivable sin, they can rightly be shown that the fact that they are worrying about it is the strongest evidence that they have not committed it. The context, however, shows a more precise possibility for the exegesis of the passage. The sin is called, in Mark's version, 'an *aeonian* sin' – a sin relating to the aeon to come. The works of Jesus are, as works of the Spirit, works of the age to come; and, understandably, the man who rejects them and calls them evil will not have a place in that aeon. An eschatological context may be the clue to the meaning.

In the non-Marcan version the main issue is the same as in the Marcan. But it includes also the puzzling contrast between blasphemy against the Spirit and blasphemy against the Son of Man. It is of course possible that there has been confusion in the tradition between 'sons of men' and 'Son of Man'. Otherwise the clue to the meaning may be that lack of belief in the claims of the Messiah may be less grave than the moral blindness of denying the Spirit's good works.

2　The other group of sayings about the Spirit concerns what the disciples will say when they are summoned before governors and magistrates. The sayings are in several contexts and are apparently derived from the non-Marcan as well as the Marcan source. In the 'eschatological discourse' in Mark, the disciples are bidden not to worry about what to say in the courts:

For it is not you who speak, but the Holy Spirit (Mark 13.11).

In the same context Luke has a variant saying, with no mention of the Holy Spirit:

For I will give you a mouth and wisdom (Luke 21.15).

In the missionary charge to the apostles in Galilee, Matthew has:

For it is not you who speak, but the Spirit of your Father speaking through you (Matt. 10.20).

And in his version of the missionary charge, Luke has:

For the Holy Spirit will teach you in that very hour what you ought to say (Luke 12.12).

There seems therefore to be good foundation for thinking that the Lord promised the disciples divine help in time of persecution, and it is at least possible that he mentioned the specific help of the Holy Spirit. Whatever precise language was used the teaching prefigures the teaching in the Fourth Gospel that after the Lord's departure the disciples will have divine help in their witness in the world.

Is the paucity of sayings of our Lord about the Holy Spirit, within the synoptic tradition, surprising? Certainly it is an instance of a primitive perspective surviving in the tradition of his teaching. The question has been asked, why did Jesus say little about the Spirit in connection with his own mission?[6] It is the kind of question to which any answer will be hazardous. Perhaps reticence about the Spirit was in line with the reticence of Jesus about his own person and claim. Perhaps also to speak of the Spirit would encourage the cruder existing ideas about it, whereas a new and more inward concept of the Spirit would come only when the mission of Jesus was fulfilled.

The same considerations may account for the reticence of Jesus about the role of the Spirit in the future. The coming of the Spirit, like the return of the Son of Man in glory, belonged to the eschatology. Only in that context would its meaning be grasped. 'Indeed the whole conception of Spirit must needs be baptized into the death of Christ. Calvary was the only gateway to Pentecost.'[7]

St Luke: Nazareth, Jerusalem, Rome

It would be fair to describe the two books written by
St Luke – the Gospel and the Acts of the Apostles – as
together the drama of the Holy Spirit. In the story of
the conception and birth of the Messiah the work of
the Holy Spirit is presented as the creation of a new
era in history. In the epistle in the synagogue of
Nazareth the Galilean ministry is introduced as the
fulfilment of Isaiah's words, 'The Spirit of the Lord is
upon me.' Filled with Holy Spirit the Messiah teaches
and heals with authority and power; and after the
resurrection he bids the apostles stay in Jerusalem
until power comes upon them. On the day of Pentecost
the exalted Jesus pours Holy Spirit upon the Church,
and the subsequent story sees the Church working in
the power of the Spirit at every stage of the progress of
the gospel from Jerusalem to Rome. With his artistry
in words and his width of sympathy St Luke sometimes describes Spirit in the Hebraic way as invading
and inspiring men and women, but more often he
writes of Spirit as indwelling and filling them. If the
latter usage is Hellenistic in form,[1] it also brings out
the note of fulfilment in Jesus Christ who possesses and
dispenses the gift.

THE CONCEPTION AND BIRTH
OF JESUS

The Messiah is coming; prophecy is returning. That is
the atmosphere of St Luke's story of the birth of John

the Baptist and of Jesus. Not only is it foretold that John 'will be filled with the Holy Spirit, even from his mother's womb' (1.15) and, receiving the role of the prophet 'will go before him in the spirit and power of Elijah' (1.17), but the scene is filled with figures uttering prophecies with joy and expectancy. Elizabeth, filled with the Spirit, greets Mary and Mary responds with the words of the Magnificat. Zechariah, filled with the Spirit, speaks the Benedictus. And later, the aged Simeon, inspired by the Spirit, comes to the temple and, with the child in his arms, says his Nunc dimittis. Anna, a prophetess, bears her part.

Prophecy has revived, for the goal of prophecy is imminent. He who is to be born will be the Davidic king, whose kingdom will last for ever. In these biblical terms the birth of Jesus is proclaimed and acclaimed.

The supreme action of the Holy Spirit is, however, in the conception and birth of him who is to be the Messiah. The angel visits Mary and predicts that she will bear a son who will reign with an everlasting kingdom. And when Mary says, 'How can this be, since I have no husband?' the angel replies:

> The Holy Spirit will come upon you, and the power of the Most High will overshadow you; therefore the child to be born will be called holy, the Son of God (Luke 1.35).

The imagery of overshadowing, *episkiazei*, is biblical and powerful. It tells of an act of new creation, recalling the first creation when the Spirit brooded over the waters (Gen. 1.2) and recalling also the divine glory overshadowing the tabernacle (Exod. 40.34). Irrespective of the question of a physical miracle accompanying it, the birth of the Saviour is indeed a creation, a coming of God into history. St Luke conveys this in the imagery of the story.

In the movement of St Luke's narrative the promise of the overshadowing by the Spirit is the angel's answer to Mary's bewilderment because she has no husband. The conception of a Son is thus the specific miracle in St Luke's mind. It is unlikely that the manuscript which lacks verse 34, 'how can this be, since I have no husband?' gives the correct text, for without that verse the careful Lucan parallelism between verses 18–20 and verses 34–5 would disappear and we would be left with a *non sequitur* narrative. If St Luke is intending to write literal history, the story is probably derived from Mary herself.

If St Luke is writing poetically in the manner of Jewish *halachah*, there is no less an event behind the poetry. In the birth of Jesus, the Holy Spirit was powerfully working in the coming of a new era.[2]

THE MINISTRY

We have already seen how all three synoptists present the baptism of Jesus as the occasion when his Sonship was proclaimed and Holy Spirit came upon him. In St Luke's account it is mentioned, characteristically, that Jesus was 'praying'; and in a text preserved in one of the Latin versions the Spirit descended 'into him', *eis auton*, a reading which accords with Luke's idea of Spirit. Jesus is 'full of the Holy Spirit' when he leaves the Jordan. After the temptation in the desert he returns to Galilee 'in the power of the Spirit' (Luke 4.14).

The role of the Spirit is further emphasized by the placing of the preaching in the synagogue at Nazareth at the beginning of the ministry. For that preaching begins with the reading of Isaiah 61.

> The Spirit of the Lord is upon me, because he has anointed me to preach good news to the poor. He has sent me to proclaim release to the captives and recovering of sight to the blind, to set at liberty those who are oppressed, to proclaim the acceptable year of the Lord (Luke 4.18–19).

These words, says Jesus, are today being fulfilled. In the power of the Spirit the Messiah's mission of deliverance begins. The people of Nazareth reject it, and their action foreshadows its rejection by the Jews and its acceptance in the Gentile world.

St Luke is a little less reticent than the other synoptists in mentioning sayings concerning the Spirit, and there are several of these, no doubt ascribable to Luke's editing (e.g. Matt. 7.11, 'good things'; Luke 11.13, 'the Holy Spirit'). And speaking to the apostles after the resurrection Jesus makes the one prediction of Pentecost which the synoptist tradition contains:

> Behold, I send the promise of my Father upon you; but stay in the city, until you are clothed with power from on high (Luke 24.49).

Thus the drama moves from Jordan back to Nazareth, and from Nazareth on to Jerusalem, with the promise that it will pass thence to the uttermost parts of the earth. The story of the ministry is seen as the fulfilment of the prophecies of the angel before the birth, and as the prelude to the powers of the Spirit in the apostolic age.

THE DAY OF PENTECOST

It has been thought by some modern scholars that the narratives in Acts about the early days of the Church in Jerusalem were derived by St Luke from several sources, and that there are some doublets in the accounts. It is possible on this hypothesis that the same event of the outpouring of the Holy Spirit lies behind both the narrative about the day of Pentecost in chapter 2 and the episode described in chapter 4:

> And when they had prayed, the place in which they were gathered together was shaken; and they were all filled with the Holy Spirit and spoke the word of God with boldness (Acts 4.31).

Be that as it may, these three clauses correspond to what the other narrative describes on the day of Pentecost – the violent convulsion, the gift of the Spirit, the boldness of speech.[3]

The account of the events at Pentecost tells of the end of the waiting. Holy Spirit comes upon the company of the believers in a way which affects profoundly their subsequent life as a community: prophetic speech, joy, fellowship, conversions – all follow the outpouring, both immediately and in the coming days and months. A new age is here. Here is St Luke's narrative:

> When the day of Pentecost had come, they were all together in one place. And suddenly a sound came from heaven like the rush of a mighty wind, and it filled all the house where they were sitting. And there appeared to them tongues of fire, distributed and resting on each one of them. And they were all

filled with the Holy Spirit and began to speak in other tongues, as the Spirit gave them utterance.

Now there were dwelling in Jerusalem Jews, devout men from every nation under heaven. And at this sound the multitude came together, and they were bewildered, because each one heard them speaking in his own language. And they were amazed and wondered, saying, 'Are not all these who are speaking Galileans? And how is it that we hear, each of us in his own native language? Parthians and Medes and Elamites and residents of Mesopotamia, Judea and Cappadocia, Pontus and Asia, Phrygia and Pamphylia, Egypt and the parts of Libya belonging to Cyrene, and visitors from Rome, both Jews and proselytes, Cretans and Arabians, we hear them telling in our own tongues the mighty works of God.' And all were amazed and perplexed, saying to one another, 'What does this mean?' But others mocking said, 'They are filled with new wine' (Acts 2.1–13).

St Luke is telling the story so as to depict at the outset the universal range of the Church's mission, as indeed he had hinted at the universal range of the Messiah's mission in the scene in the synagogue at Nazareth. The little company of the disciples was keeping the festival of Pentecost. This was originally an agrarian 'feast of weeks', but it had come in Judaism to be a commemoration of the giving of the divine law at Mount Sinai, an event linked with the imagery of fire and wind. On this feast of Pentecost there happens a vivid manifestation of the invading power of God, in familiar symbols. Perhaps the mention that the Spirit 'filled all the house' recalls also the account of the vision of Isaiah in the temple in Isaiah 6. Overwhelmed by what they see and hear, the little company of disciples are convinced that Holy Spirit has come upon them.

The Jews of the dispersion who were present would come from many nations; and St Luke sees in the series a map of the places from which they come, circling across the Middle East and the Mediterranean world, from the Persian Gulf to the farther parts of North Africa, a symbol of the world into which the gospel is going to be carried. With this map in his mind's eye he describes the disciples as speaking in 'other tongues', a sign of the universality of the Church's mission. This astounds those present, who – as the narrative stands – are witnessing a miraculous gift of speech in foreign languages. But while St Luke's dramatic picture is a powerful meditation on the universality of the gospel, in counterpart to the confusion and division brought by the episode of the tower of Babel, if we probe into the likely event behind the story we may think it probable that what happened was the *glossolalia* or 'speaking with tongues', the ecstatic kind of utterance described elsewhere in the Acts and in the Epistles. We then picture the apostolic company being swept 'out of themselves' into an ecstatic outburst of speech. This would indeed fit the writer's comment that they appeared to the onlookers to be drunk.

No, it was not drunkenness; and St Peter now tells the crowd what it really was in what was perhaps the speech of a lifetime. His theme was this: we are not drunk, it is too early in the day for that (one of St Luke's little touches of humour which recur in his writings); but the prophecy of Joel about the outpouring of Spirit on the day of the Lord has today been fulfilled. St Peter cites Joel 2.28–32, with its picture of Spirit outpoured, of prophesyings, dreams and visions, and portents in heaven and earth; and St Luke adds to the quotation a reference to 'prophesyings'. But how and why has this outpouring come? It is Jesus who is the author of the day's event, Jesus whom the Jews crucified but God raised up. The death of Jesus by crucifixion, though contrived in wickedness, lay within the agelong purpose of God and so did the resurrection that followed. Then comes the climax of St Peter's speech:

> This Jesus God raised up, and of that we are all witnesses. Being therefore exalted at the right hand of God, and having received from the Father the promise of the Holy Spirit, he has poured out this which you see and hear ... Let all the house of Israel know assuredly that God has made him both Lord and Christ, this Jesus whom you crucified (Acts 2.32–3; 36).

So the Spirit, poured out on this day, is the gift of the crucified and exalted Jesus. The Spirit is the Spirit of Jesus. That is the revolution in the concept of Spirit which appears in the early Church. Whether St Luke is recording the gist of St Peter's speech accurately or no, this teaching, that the Spirit is the Spirit of the exalted Jesus, is – as we shall see – well attested in the Pauline Epistles. Jesus, in his death and resurrection, is the author of the vivid experience among the believers to which the name Holy Spirit was given.

Cut to the heart by St Peter's words, many ask what they should do; and St Peter's final word to them is this:

Repent, and be baptized every one of you in the name of Jesus Christ for the forgiveness of your sins; and you shall receive the gift of the Holy Spirit. For the promise is to you and to your children and to all that are far off, every one whom the Lord our God calls to him (Acts 2.38–9).

Conversions followed. About 3,000 people were baptized that day; and subsequently they devoted themselves 'to the apostles' teaching and fellowship, to the breaking of bread and the prayers' (Acts 2.42).

So the Church sets out on its mission. It is a mission, like that of the Messiah, in the power of the Spirit. The drama which St Luke has traced from Nazareth to Jordan and from Jordan to Jerusalem now moves on towards Rome.

THE SPIRIT AND THE CHURCH

After Pentecost the Spirit is active in many aspects of the Christian community. The Spirit's power is specially noticed in preaching, in prophecy, in boldness of witness, in joy, and in the making of decisions by the apostles. From a summary of the allusions to the Spirit after the day of Pentecost the reader will see the picture which the Book of Acts presents and some of the problems of interpretation which are posed.

Peter preaches, full of the Holy Spirit (Acts 4.8).

The place where the apostles pray is shaken, and they are filled with the Holy Spirit and speak the word with boldness (4.31–4).

The apostles are witnesses, and so is the Holy Spirit (5.32).

The seven are chosen, as men full of the Holy Spirit and of wisdom (6.3).

Stephen, full of the Holy Spirit, sees the vision of Jesus in glory (7.55).

The Spirit comes to converts in Samaria after they receive the laying on of hands of apostles from Jerusalem, with prayer (8.18).

The Spirit tells Philip what to do (8.29).

The Spirit carries Philip from one place to another (8.39).

Ananias is sent to Saul so that he may recover sight and be filled with the Holy Spirit (9.17).

The Church has the fear of the Lord and the consolation of the Holy Spirit (9.31).

The Spirit tells Peter the meaning of his dream (10.19).

People in Caesarea give evidence of the Holy Spirit by speaking with tongues and praising God, and Peter says: 'Can any one forbid water for baptizing these people who have received the Holy Spirit just as we have?' (10.47).

The Spirit prompts the Church in Antioch to commission Barnabas and Saul for a mission (13.1–4).

It seemed good to the Holy Spirit and to us (15.28).

The Spirit forbids the apostles to preach in Asia (16.6).

Some disciples in Ephesus are baptized and when Paul lays his hands on them they receive the Holy Spirit and speak in tongues and prophesy (19.1–6).

The Holy Spirit witnesses to Paul that bonds and afflictions await him (20.23).

Agabus reports a prophecy made by the Holy Spirit (21.10).

The Holy Spirit spoke through the prophet Isaiah (28.25).

In all these ways the Book of Acts tells of the role of the Spirit in the expansion of the Church. There is throughout a strong emphasis upon the power of the Spirit in preaching and prophecy, and we shall find this emphasis strongly corroborated in the Pauline Epistles. We notice also two occasions when, on the first reception of the Holy Spirit, people speak with tongues. At Caesarea they were 'speaking in tongues and extolling God' (Acts 10.46) and at Ephesus they 'spoke with tongues and prophesied' (19.6). Our discussion of the role of speaking with tongues must await St Paul's evidence, and so must our discussion of the relation of Holy Spirit to the sacrament of baptism. Here we note only two emphatic instances of a link between the sacrament of baptism and the gift of the Spirit. One is on the day of Pentecost (2.38) and the other is at Ephesus (19.5–6).

To whom, however, is the gospel to be preached? St Luke draws out the stages by which the apostles in Jerusalem were led to grasp the full implications of the universality of the gospel. Clinging to the idea that Jesus had come 'to restore the kingdom to Israel' (Acts 1.6), they were led to know first that Gentiles may be converted and baptized, and later that Gentiles thus converted need not be burdened with the keeping of the whole law (15.19–20). It is here that we see the significance of the episode in Caesarea, where the falling of the Holy Spirit upon those who believed the gospel convinces St Peter that it is right for them to be baptized (10.41–8). It seems that St Luke is not describing 'norms' for the Church's discipline so much as stages in the Spirit's education of the apostles in the universality of the gospel. So the drama moves on until the day when St Paul is seen preaching the gospel from

43

his own hired dwelling in Rome.

The theologian finds in the Acts of the Apostles both the distinctive emphasis in St Luke which runs through both his volumes, and also testimony to more widespread thought and teaching about the Spirit. The Spirit is sometimes described as an invasive power in the manner of the Hebrew *ruach*, sometimes as a power which fills the recipient who makes it his continuing possession. This in turn illustrates a tension between two aspects of the Church which recurs in the apostolic age and in subsequent Christian history.

The historian asks how far St Luke may be obscuring the facts by recording them in the light of his own theological trend and dramatic purpose. That he sees the rise of Christianity as a drama of the Holy Spirit is clear. But having noticed how relatively little of this interpretation he presses into his editing of the synoptic tradition, we are given confidence in his story. So too we shall be given confidence when we see how largely his account of the liveliness of the early Church by the power of the Spirit is corroborated by the first-hand testimony of St Paul's letters.

4

The Witness of St Paul

1

No writer of the first century tells us more than St Paul of the belief of the early Christians in the Holy Spirit, and of what the Holy Spirit meant to them as well as to him, from the time of their conversion onwards. At the same time St Paul had his own lines of thought about this, as about every, part of Christian belief. In particular we find him in some of his letters struggling to use ideas and expressions of a gnostic type of religion for his exposition of the Christian faith, and at the same time combating some grave misconceptions of Christianity to which his exposition might have given plausibility.

St Paul was sure that the Spirit was powerfully at work in the preaching of the gospel and in the conversion of those who responded to it. He writes of this in one of his earliest letters:

> We know, brethren beloved by God, that he has chosen you; for our gospel came to you not only in word, but also in power and in the Holy Spirit and with full conviction ... And you became imitators of us and of the Lord, for you received the word in much affliction, with joy inspired by the Holy Spirit (1 Thess. 1.4-6).

The preaching which led to conversion did not rely upon human artifice but upon the power of the Holy Spirit. It was thus that it brought conviction to the hearers:

My speech and my message were not in plausible words of wisdom, but in demonstration of the Spirit and power (1 Cor. 2.4).

Indeed, looking back upon his mission to the Gentiles, St Paul felt the whole story to be evidence of the Spirit's power in both the giving and the receiving:

In Christ Jesus, then, I have reason to be proud of my work for God. For I will not venture to speak of anything except what Christ has wrought through me to win obedience from the Gentiles, by word and deed, by the power of signs and wonders, by the power of the Holy Spirit (Rom. 15.17–19).

Beginning their Christian life in the Holy Spirit, the converts in every place would understand subsequent injunctions of the apostle to walk in the Spirit (Gal. 5.16), to be led by the Spirit (Rom. 8.14), or to live according to the Spirit (Rom. 8.5), as well as language describing the Spirit as sovereign 'Lord' (2 Cor. 3.17).

While the variety of language about Spirit witnesses to the large role of Spirit in the Christian experience, it poses questions about the concepts which the language expresses, and the respective place of Jewish, Greek, and distinctively Christian elements in the thought.

2

There is the contrast which we have noticed in other New Testament contexts between Spirit as a power which invades human lives in the manner of *ruach* in the Old Testament, and Spirit as gifts to persons to possess like a substance or fluid within them. We have seen that the latter is prominent in St Luke's thought, but it is doubtful whether we should regard it as a specially Hellenistic usage.[1]

The Stoic idea of Spirit was a kind of divine substance indwelling the world and giving it unity and rationality, and we have seen the possibility that this idea infiltrated the thought of Greek-speaking Jews about divine Spirit and Wisdom. But while there is a superficial parallel between the Stoic idea and St Paul's concept of the Spirit indwelling the Church as the body of Christ, we shall find in a later chapter that in the Pauline concept the Spirit is dynamically related to the risen Christ. It is noteworthy that in St Paul's writings Spirit is never mentioned in relation to the cosmos.[2]

In yet another kind of language Spirit is the atmosphere, the realm, indeed almost the air, in which Christians have come to live. This is indeed akin to the gnostic idea of the spiritual realm to which human spirits, receiving salvation through gnosis or knowledge, are to be delivered. But St Paul's idea of the new realm is very different from the gnostic, as it is dominated by the Hebrew and Christian eschatology. Spirit is the *arrabon* or promise of the age to come, where Christ is in glory.

We need, however, to probe more deeply into the relation of St Paul to gnosticism. The connection between gnosticism and early Christianity is a field about which there are still many uncertainties. While it is unlikely that the developed gnostic systems which confronted the Church in the second century go back to the apostolic age, it is certain that they had their precursors in religious trends in the earlier period. Certain ideas about spirit, matter, knowledge, and salvation, identified as gnostic, existed within Hellenistic

Judaism, within pagan Greek sects and within Christian communities; and it is evident that some Christian teachers used gnostic ideas and phrases as a medium for the exposition of the Christian gospel. While this could aid the presentation of the Christian faith in a cultural setting different from its original one, it ran the risk of some grave misconceptions which would in turn have to be repudiated.[3]

St Paul for his part seems to have been ready to use terms which Greek converts would understand, and to adopt an element of gnostic vocabulary. To become 'perfect' and 'spiritual' were gnostic ideas, and St Paul could use them, though with a difference, as the first two chapters of 1 Corinthians show. Again, the idea of invisible powers of evil who held the world in bondage, was also congenial to St Paul, and he writes of the 'beggarly elemental spirits' (Gal. 4.9), the 'rulers of this age' (1 Cor. 2.8), and the 'principalities' and 'powers' (Rom. 8.38). But St Paul did more than borrow phrases. It seems that he used one of the central gnostic 'patterns' in telling the story of salvation: the myth of a divine redeemer who comes to earth to bring salvation to mankind and then returns to heaven (cf. Phil. 2.6–11; 2 Cor. 8.9; and Eph. 4.8–11). Indeed this imagery could give true expression to the relation of Jesus Christ to God and to the world.

Yet the basic gnostic ideas about the world and about the content of salvation were deeply at variance with the Christian gospel. The gnostics held that the material world was evil, a prison in which spiritual beings were trapped; spirit was held to be the true world; and salvation meant rescuing the spirits of human beings and uniting them with the divine spirit which is their proper destiny. It is by *knowledge* that this union with the divine spirit can be realized; and it can happen here and now for those who are initiated into the way of salvation. There is therefore no room for a futurist eschatology or for a salvation for the human body, or for a Son of God who came in the flesh. If St Paul and, later, St John were able to use some of the phrases of the gnostics and some of their mythology, the differences were – as we shall see – profound.

It is in the Epistles to the Church in Corinth that we see St Paul grappling with the gnostic problem, and in so doing he draws out powerfully the Christian meaning of the Holy Spirit. Some of the Christians in Corinth had, it seems, misunderstood parts of St Paul's teaching and twisted words like spirit, knowledge, wisdom, perfect, away from their Christian meaning. We do not know whether St Paul may have given cause for this by unguarded language. But the letter known as 1 Corinthians shows him taking the opportunity to relate these key words firmly to the cross of Christ, and to show that the Spirit is the Spirit of Christ crucified.

In the first two chapters the picture unfolds itself. Here is a Church full of spiritual gifts, including wisdom, knowledge, and eloquence (1 Cor. 1.5–7) and yet deeply torn by quarrelsome cliques. In this setting St Paul insists that divine wisdom is supremely seen in the cross of Christ, that the men who had preached the cross were not nobly born intellectuals, and that their method was not lofty eloquence but 'in demonstration of the Spirit and power' (2.4). There are indeed those who are spiritually mature, but it is a maturity bestowed by the Holy Spirit, for

what no eye has seen, nor ear heard, nor the heart of

man conceived, what God has prepared for those who love him, God has revealed to us through the Spirit. For the Spirit searches everything, even the depths of God. For what person knows a man's thoughts except the spirit of the man which is in him? So also no one comprehends the thoughts of God except the Spirit of God. Now we have received not the spirit of the world, but the Spirit which is from God, that we might understand the gifts bestowed on us by God. And we impart this in words not taught by human wisdom but taught by the Spirit, interpreting spiritual truths to those who possess the Spirit (2.9–13).

Thus the Spirit conveys divine thoughts and understanding to the Christians and enables them to perceive, discriminate, and respond. Two realms are contrasted, the realm of the 'psychic' man, the natural man, the man who has missed the impact of Holy Spirit – and the realm of the 'spiritual' man. And many who might think themselves 'spiritual' on account of their knowledge are in fact merely natural or unspiritual. For,

the unspiritual [psychic] man does not receive the gifts of the Spirit of God, for they are folly to him, and he is not able to understand them because they are spiritually discerned. The spiritual man judges all things, but is himself to be judged by no one. 'For who has known the mind of the Lord so as to instruct him?' But we have the mind of Christ (2.14–16).

Such is the contrast. The key to the understanding of the new and spiritual realm has been the cross, whose wisdom and power are missed by the wisdom and power of the world. But those who, humbled and made wise by the cross, belong to the new order, have gifts of wisdom and knowledge. As the precondition of entrance into the new order is the cross of Christ, so its outcome is to share in 'the mind of Christ'. Elsewhere we learn that the mind of Christ is the mind of one who did not grasp at prerogative but poured himself out, taking the form of a servant (Phil. 2.5–7).

St Paul returns to the theme of the Holy Spirit in chapter 12, when he deals with the problems concerning spiritual gifts and the disturbance caused by some of them in the Christian assemblies. We will consider this in a later chapter, within the subject of the Christian fellowship. It will now be appropriate to pass on to chapter 15, for as 1 Corinthians begins by showing the relation of the Holy Spirit to the cross, so it ends by showing the relation of the Holy Spirit to the resurrection.

There were in Corinth those who denied that there will be a future resurrection of Christians who had died. The denial may have had behind it an unwillingness to believe that the body can be saved, or can be of relevance within the life of salvation; and a belief that the true destiny of Christians is a union of human spirits with divine Spirit, here and now, with no room for an 'eschatology'. In answer, St Paul affirms that Jesus Christ was raised on the third day, according to the tradition he had received, and he was raised so as to be the source of new life to those who were united to him. This new life will be bodily as well as spiritual, and in the future resurrection the Christian will have not indeed the identical flesh and blood of his present existence but a 'spiritual body' related to the present body as plant is related to seed, with both change and continuity. Such is St Paul's familiar argument. If there is no resurrection of the dead then Christ cannot have been raised and we are still in the old order of sin.

It is near the climax of his argument that St Paul draws out the role of Spirit.[4] He contrasts man's physical body as part of the natural order with man's body as it will become by the power of Christ's resurrection – his 'spiritual body'. With this contrast there is linked another contrast, between Adam who is no more than 'living' and Christ who is not only 'living' but 'life-giving':

It is sown a physical body, it is raised a spiritual body. If there is a physical body, there is also a spiritual body. Thus it is written, 'The first man Adam became a living being'; the last Adam became a life-giving spirit. But it is not the spiritual which is first but the physical, and then the spiritual. The first man was from the earth, a man of dust; the second man is from heaven. As was the man of dust, so are those who are of the dust; and as is the man from heaven, so are those who are of heaven. Just as we have borne the image of the man of dust, we shall also bear the image of the man of heaven (1 Cor. 15.44–9).

To unravel this passage is to see deeper into St Paul's thought about the Spirit.

The contrasts are clear: the natural body, the spiritual body; the one is akin to Adam, the other is akin to Christ; the one is from the dust, the other is, like Christ himself, 'from heaven'. Now the concept of the man from heaven was familiar in contemporary religion, both Greek and Jewish, and indeed C. K.

Barrett in the note in his commentary on 1 Corinthians says that a hundred parallels can be cited! Superficially it might seem that the idea of Christ as 'from heaven' would be congenial to gnostics as a heavenly saviour from a material world. But, no! Christ the man from heaven is one who had been born in the flesh and crucified in weakness, one who had shared in man's whole life in body, soul, and spirit. It was this Jesus who at his resurrection *became* life-giving Spirit. The power of Holy Spirit is the power of the heavenly Christ who was raised as the one who had been crucified.

In the Epistle to the Romans, St Paul is no less emphatic that the Spirit of the Risen Christ is the Spirit of the Christ who had lived and died. The Gospel is described at the outset as

the gospel concerning his Son, who was descended from David according to the flesh and designated Son of God in power according to the Spirit of holiness by his resurrection from the dead (Rom. 1.3–4).

And, whereas in 1 Corinthians 15 the figure of the second Adam is Christ risen from the dead, in Romans 5 the figure of the second Adam is Christ whose obedience in his life and death redresses the disobedience of the first Adam. While in the unfolding of Christian doctrine it is the resurrection which first has prominence, it is from Jesus in his life and death as well as resurrection that the power of Holy Spirit flows. For all the novelty of his thought and language St Paul is never far from the teaching which St Peter gave in his speech on the day of Pentecost.

By his readiness to use language and imagery of a gnostic kind, St Paul was able to expound the gospel in a setting wider than the Jewish milieu in which it was first presented. But he could do this only because he clings to the tradition that Jesus had revealed God in his historical life and death and resurrection and that from these events the power of Holy Spirit had been realized. The more that we see of the varieties in early Christianity the more apparent is the underlying unity.

3

How did St Paul think of the relation between the Spirit, God, and Christ?

The Spirit is, for St Paul, emphatically the Spirit of God. The recurrence of the phrase shows the continuity of his thought with the Old Testament belief that Spirit is God's activity. But it is no less clear that the Spirit is the powerful and intimate impact of the risen Christ upon the believers. Indeed so close is the Spirit to Christ and to God that much of the language scarcely suggests the idea of a separate personal being. The impersonal imagery of wind, fire, and water continues.

Yet language of a more intimately personal kind appears. The Spirit acts as he 'wills' in the distributing of gifts (1 Cor. 12.11), the Spirit 'guides' (Rom. 8.14) and, above all, the Spirit prays and intercedes (Gal. 4.6; Rom. 8.26–9). Trinitarian language appears, not in metaphysical statements but in accounts of Christian experience. Experience lies behind the blessing at the end of 2 Corinthians, 'the grace of the Lord Jesus Christ and the love of God and the fellowship of the Holy Spirit' (2 Cor. 13.14). A trinitarian pattern appears in St Paul's account of the Christian life in

Romans 5.1–8, and in Ephesians 2.18 the access of the Christians is described as through Jesus Christ 'in one Spirit to the Father'.

It has been held that St Paul, at least sometimes, identified the Spirit and the risen Christ. We have seen how strongly 1 Corinthians 15.45, 'the last Adam became a life-giving spirit', suggests this. On the other hand it is a mistake to claim 2 Corinthians 3.17, 'now the Lord is the Spirit', as evidence for an identification, for, as we shall see in the next chapter, the context suggests not an identity but a parallelism between an Old Testament episode and a present experience. The issue was well summarized by Dr Eduard Schweizer in these words:

Paul shares with Judaism and with the early Christian Church the conception of the Spirit as the gift and power of the last age. His concern is not to replace the concept of 'power' by the concept of 'person', but to show that this power is not an obscure 'something' but is the way and manner in which the Lord of the Church is present. For that reason the Spirit can be placed on a level with the Lord, or subordinated to him, quite indifferently. For that reason also, Paul can occasionally use God, Lord, and Spirit interchangeably, simply because their encounter with the believer always takes the same form.[5]

While the impact of the Holy Spirit upon the Christians is inseparable from the impact of the risen Christ, there is evidence of distinction between the relation of the Christians to Christ and their relation to the Spirit. Scholars have noticed three kinds of distinction.

There is the distinction between the Christians having 'communion' with Christ and their experiencing 'possession' by the Spirit, and the two relationships deepen and illuminate each other. This was the theme of a well-known essay by Dr K. E. Kirk.[6] Another distinction was convincingly drawn out by Father Lionel Thornton:

> Christ and the Spirit dwell in the Christian soul, but act in the same way. Christ is the indwelling content of the Christian life. He is being 'formed' in us ... we are to be 'conformed to his image' ... and we are to 'grow up into him'. Spirit is the quickening cause, the indwelling of Christ is the effect of that cause.[7]

The truth of that distinction becomes convincing when we try to reverse the language. More recently a distinction between the relationships has been suggested by C. F. D. Moule. 'Although', he writes,

> these are exceptions and Paul's usage is not wholly consistent, nevertheless there is a discernible tendency not to say indifferently 'we in Christ' and 'Christ in us' but to speak of Christians as in Christ and of the Holy Spirit as in Christians. To be a Christian is to be incorporated in Christ and to have the Spirit of Christ within oneself.[8]

So the language about the Holy Spirit tells of both the power and the intimacy of God's revelation of himself through Jesus Christ. The response of the believers to God's action towards them is enabled by God's action within them. God within responds to God beyond, as the Spirit prays within them and mingles his prayers with theirs (Rom. 8.15–17, 26–7).

5

St Paul: The Spirit and the Christian Life

What did the Holy Spirit mean in the lives of the early Christians? This chapter and the next will explore this, with St Paul as our chief guide. If the headings of the two chapters serve for convenience, the division of the themes is inevitably a little arbitrary.

THE NEW AGE

The Holy Spirit is, in the mind of the early Christians, the power of the age to come, an age which they both await expectantly and already enjoy by anticipation. Two single words of metaphor express this. One is *arrabon*, the first instalment, or guarantee, or 'promissory note' of an inheritance to come (2 Cor. 1.22; Eph. 1.13, 4.30). The other is *aparche*, the first-fruits to the future world (Rom. 8.25). But nowhere is this aspect of the Spirit more vividly seen than in the Epistle to the Hebrews. The writer, whose name is unknown to us, in recalling what it means when people are initiated as Christians, describes them as

> those who have once been enlightened, who have tasted the heavenly gift, and have become partakers of the Holy Spirit, and have tasted the goodness of the word of God and the powers of the age to come (Heb. 6.4–5).

'Heavenly gift', 'Holy Spirit', 'age to come': it is into this that Christians are initiated. Holy Spirit keeps

alive in them the awareness of a heavenly calling and
the beginning of a heavenly life.

It helps us to understand this eschatological pattern
if we glance at the concept of glory in the apostolic
writings. Jesus had predicted a coming in glory beyond
the passion (Mark 8.38, 13.26), and his transfiguration
in the presence of three disciples on the Mount was a
glimpse in advance of the glory to be (cf. 1 Pet. 5.1).
The early Christians believed that Jesus was now in
heavenly glory (Acts 3.21, 7.35; Col. 3.1; 1 Pet. 1.21; 1
Tim. 3.16). Believing Jesus to be in glory the Christians are looking forward to a day when they will
themselves share in it. Past, present, and future are
united in the words which St Paul writes to the Colossians:

> If then you have been raised with Christ, seek the
> things that are above, where Christ is, seated at the
> right hand of God. Set your minds on things that are
> above, not on things that are on earth. For you have
> died, and your life is hid with Christ in God. When
> Christ who is our life appears, then you also will
> appear with him in glory (Col. 3.1–4).

Bengel's famous comment on these words is worth recalling: 'The world does not know the Christians, and
the Christians do not indeed know themselves.' Such is
the bewilderment of Christian existence. In this world,
heirs of another; possessing the risen Christ, whose life
in them is invisible; but awaiting a day of glory when
the secret now hidden within them will be seen.

Yet, the Christians find the glory within them
already, and not least does this happen in their experience of suffering. We shall later be dwelling upon the
concluding part of Romans 8 where the Christians, in

the midst of the frustration of the cosmos, look forward to the future, knowing that

> the sufferings of this present time are not worth comparing with the glory that is to be revealed (Rom. 8.18),

but find that this glory is already theirs, for it is true of all kinds of suffering and disaster that

> in all these things we are more than conquerors through him who loved us (Rom. 8.37).

It is the Spirit making intercession within the Christians who enables this (Rom. 8.26–7). This theme recurs in the First Epistle of Peter. Here the writer tells Christians in Asia Minor that if persecution comes to them, they need not fear. Indeed,

> if you are reproached for the name of Christ, you are blessed, because the spirit of glory and of God rests upon you (1 Pet. 4.14).

Here too it is the Spirit who works what can fairly be called the transfiguration of suffering.

In the third chapter of 2 Corinthians St Paul describes in vivid imagery the Christians' experience of Spirit and glory. He begins by contrasting the old covenant and the new. The old was based on the law, the new is based on the Spirit. Religion based on law becomes formal and deadening, but the Spirit is life-giving. The difference is not, like the modern idea, between 'inward' and 'outward', but between a life based upon rule and a life quickened by the power of Holy Spirit, for 'the written code kills, but the Spirit gives life'. Then follows the contrast between the glory of the old covenant and the glory of the new covenant, worked out in a quaint parallelism between the experience of Moses and the Israelites at Mount Sinai and the present experience of the Christians. When Moses descended from Sinai, he had a veil over his face so that the Israelites should not be dazzled by the divine radiance, but when he turned to the Lord he removed the veil. Today, Jews who reject the gospel cannot see the divine glory, for a veil rests over their minds when they read the law. But when any of them 'turns to the Lord', as a convert to the gospel, the veil is removed. And to 'turn to the Lord' means, in the new dispensation, to turn to the Spirit – for 'Lord' in the one imagery is paralleled by 'spirit' in the other. The Spirit is the source of freedom, and the power whereby lives are changed into Christ's own likeness:

> Now the Lord is the Spirit, and where the Spirit of the Lord is, there is freedom. And we all, with unveiled face, beholding the glory of the Lord, are being changed into his likeness from one degree of glory to another; for this comes from the Lord who is the Spirit (2 Cor. 3.17–18).

Such is the splendid climax of St Paul's argument. In contrast with the scanty access to the divine glory in the time of Moses, there is now the unrestricted access for all Christians, an access leading to the vision of Christ and to transformation into his likeness. In verse 18 the Greek verb includes the notion of a mirror, and can fairly be translated either 'beholding as in a mirror' or 'reflecting as in a mirror'. Though 'reflecting' was preferred by Chrysostom in the ancient world and by the R.S.V. in the modern, the context favours 'beholding'. Here is one of the great pictures of the Christian life: the Christians see God's glory mirrored in Jesus Christ, and while seeing they are made like him. Parts of the picture recur in Romans 12.2, 'be transformed by the renewal of your mind', and in 1 John 3.2, 'we shall be like him, for we shall see him as he is'. While St Paul's language has some resemblance to an idea of deification, he guards against that idea by introducing the word 'image'. The Christians do not become the divine glory, they become like its image seen in the historical life of Jesus.

'Now the Lord is the Spirit.' Does this sentence imply an identification of the Spirit with the risen Christ? We shall probably not think so if we see that the context and the argument require putting 'Lord' in inverted commas. The Spirit truly is the equivalent of 'the Lord' in the Moses story – but the difference is one of sovereign power, the transformation of the lives of the Christians; 'This comes from the Lord who is the Spirit.' (Perhaps indeed in the closing phrase it may be right to take 'Lord', *kuriou*, as adjectival, and to render 'this comes from the Spirit who is sovereign'.) St Paul is not theorizing about the relation of God, Christ, and the Spirit; he is ascribing to Spirit a sovereignty which is divine.

It is of the apostles that St Paul is writing. But the scope of his argument widens to all Christians: 'We all, with unveiled face ...' To all Christians is offered the access, the vision, the transfiguring. It is no fancy picture. What kind of life it could mean is drawn out in the next three chapters of 2 Corinthians when St Paul recalls the sorrows and the joys of an apostle's life in a way that is indeed applicable to all Christians:

always carrying in the body the death of Jesus, so

that the life of Jesus may be manifested in our mortal flesh (2 Cor. 4.10).

No part of St Paul's writings is more down to earth than these chapters, with their picture of what Christians can endure in the service of the gospel. But another world is near, and the other-worldly context is seen as a new creation (2 Cor. 4.6, 5.17) and as the swallowing-up of the present mortality into resurrection and life (5.1–10). That is the setting of the Christian life. Its author and sustainer is the Holy Spirit (3.17; cf. 6.6).

THE CHRISTIANS IN THE WORLD

The Christian life which the Spirit sustains is no escapism. It is a life of faith and love amidst the world's strains and pressures. Two aspects of this life are specially linked with the Holy Spirit. It is a way of *holiness* and it is a way of *sonship*.

1 The idea of *holiness* finds a new emphasis in the early Church. In an Old Testament context the addition of the adjective 'holy' to the noun 'spirit' is not so very significant, for in the Old Testament 'spirit' is by definition divine, and in prophets and psalms the word 'spirit' of itself says much of what 'holy spirit' would say. None the less, holiness was a primary doctrine in the Old Testament. God's holiness is his otherness in awe and mystery, his apartness from the created world. But he is none the less a God who makes himself known to his people and demands that they shall be holy too (Exod. 19.6). The holy God is revealed through the holy nation.

In the new covenant the role of the 'holy nation' is now taken over by the Christians; they are the *ecclesia* of God, they are called to be holy, they are the elect race, the holy nation, the people for God's own possession (1 Pet. 2.9). And it is this which has a new intensity, due to the new inwardness of relationship between God and the believers which Jesus Christ has brought about, an inwardness of relationship which the Holy Spirit creates and continues. Most vividly is this seen in the language which describes the Christians not only as constituting the holy people but as being themselves personally *the holy ones*. The use of *hoi hagioi*, the holy ones, as the normal description of the Christians, brings out the new and overwhelming emphasis upon holiness in Christianity.

The salutation at the beginning of 1 Corinthians shows the new emphasis:

> ... to the church of God which is at Corinth, to those sanctified in Christ Jesus, called to be saints together with all those who in every place call on the name of our Lord Jesus Christ, both their Lord and ours (1 Cor. 1.2).

As the word Spirit now belongs closely to the risen Christ, so does the word Holy which goes with it. The plea to take seriously the call to holiness recurs in the Epistles, sometimes with the reminder that Christians must be very different from their pagan neighbours and sometimes with the thought that Christians are themselves the sacred temple of God's presence. Thus we read:

> And such were some of you. But you were washed, you were sanctified, you were justified in the name

of the Lord Jesus Christ and in the Spirit of our God (1 Cor. 6.11).

I appeal to you therefore, brethren, by the mercies of God, to present your bodies as a living sacrifice, holy and acceptable to God, which is your spiritual worship (Rom. 12.1).

... a minister of Christ Jesus to the Gentiles in the priestly service of the gospel of God, so that the offering of the Gentiles may be acceptable, sanctified by the Holy Spirit (Rom. 15.16).

... a holy temple in the Lord; in whom you also are built into it for a dwelling place of God in the Spirit (Eph. 2.21–2).

The cultic presentation of the Christian life, as the true worship and sacrifice, is less prominent in St Paul than in the Epistle to the Hebrews, where apostasy from the Christian faith is described in terrible words which show the seriousness of the issue of holiness:

... the man who has spurned the Son of God, and profaned the blood of the covenant by which he was sanctified, and outraged the Spirit of grace (Heb. 10.29).

In the Fourth Gospel we shall find the theme of the holiness of the disciples linked with the self-consecration of our Lord in his death, in the words in the prayer after the supper:

And for their sake I consecrate myself, that they also may be consecrated in truth (John 17.19).

The apartness of our Lord in his death belongs to his mission for the salvation of the world. Such too will be the apartness of the disciples. The concept of holiness is indeed revolutionized when it is linked with the glory of divine self-giving love, and with the mission of the disciples to the world.

2   So life in the Spirit is holiness. It is also *sonship*, a theme which St Paul draws out both in Galatians and in Romans.

Jesus prayed to God as Father, and he used the word *Abba*. Dr Jeremias has shown the striking originality of this language in the prayer of Jesus. 'In the literature of Palestinian Judaism no evidence has yet been found of "my Father" being used by an individual as an address to God ... It is quite unusual that Jesus should have addressed God as "my Father"; it is even more so that he should have used the dramatic form *Abba*.'[1] In Jesus' mode of address to God there was thus a rare intensive intimacy. '*Abba* as a form of address to God expresses the ultimate mystery of the mission of Jesus. He was conscious of being authorized to communicate God's revelation, because God had made himself known to him as Father (cf. Matt. 11.27).' The Sonship of Jesus was his own. In so far as the disciples came to share in it, it would be in a sonship dependent upon, and derived from, his.

It is this sonship which the Holy Spirit reproduces in the Christian believers. Two passages specially describe this.

In Galatians 4 the contrast is between the immature state of those under the law, who, though children and heirs, were in tutelage and fear, and the present privilege of a mature sonship.

So with us; when we were children, we were slaves to

the elemental spirits of the universe. But when the time had fully come, God sent forth his Son, born of woman, born under the law, to redeem those who were under the law, so that we might receive adoption as sons. And because you are sons, God has sent the Spirit of his Son into our hearts, crying, 'Abba! Father!' (Gal. 3.4–6).

In freedom the Christians made their own the intimate prayer of Jesus.

In Romans 8 the contrast is both with the state of condemnation of those who sought salvation by the keeping of the law, and with the compromised life of those who live 'after the flesh' – which means a worldly existence unresponsive to God and the age to come. Life 'according to the flesh' is really 'death', but the rule of the Spirit gives the life whose essence is sonship:

For all who are led by the Spirit of God are sons of God. For you did not receive the spirit of slavery to fall back into fear, but you have received the spirit of sonship. When we cry, 'Abba! Father!' it is the Spirit himself bearing witness with our spirit that we are children of God, and if children, then heirs, heirs of God and fellow heirs with Christ, provided we suffer with him in order that we may also be glorified with him (Rom. 8.14–17).

There seems here to be evidence that the Christians make their own the words of Jesus' own prayer to the Father. So praying, enabled by the Spirit's own prayer, they live without fear in trustful intimacy with the Father, ready to have a share in Christ's suffering, as they await their share in his glory.

3 So the Christians are called to holiness and to sonship. They do not, however, find sin once for all over-
come, for their life is one of conflict and growth. In
this conflict and growth the Spirit is their guide, and
the apostle often exhorts them to yield to his promptings and to let him complete what he has begun in
them. They must be led by the Spirit, let the Spirit
rule in their hearts, not quench the Spirit, not grieve
the Spirit, and endeavour to guard the unity of the
Spirit in the bond of peace. The conflict is variously
described. It is a conflict with sin within, and with
demonic forces without. It is described as a *conflict of
flesh and spirit.*

What meaning is to be given to the conflict of flesh
and spirit? At first glance it might suggest an antithesis between the bodily aspect of man as sinful and
the spiritual aspect of man as otherwise, for indeed
sinful impulses operate through the body (cf. Rom.
6.12). But it is fundamental in St Paul's thinking that
the body is not inherently evil and is to be raised from
death hereafter and sanctified by the Spirit now.

> The body is not meant for immorality, but for the
> Lord, and the Lord for the body. And God raised
> the Lord and will also raise us up by his power (1
> Cor. 6.13–14).

> ... he who raised Christ Jesus from the dead will
> give life to your mortal bodies also through his
> Spirit which dwells in you (Rom. 8–11).

And earlier still St Paul had told the Thessalonians of
the divine purpose for the sanctification of the entire
life of man:

> ... may your spirit and soul and body be kept sound

and blameless at the coming of our Lord Jesus Christ (1 Thess. 5.23).

In so far as St Paul had a psychology, it was very likely the idea that a human being is composed of flesh (*sarx*), soul (*psyche*), and spirit (*pneuma*), the soul denoting the faculty of life and the spirit the higher mental or moral qualities. That sin made its assaults through the flesh or body, as the 'lower' components of man, was no doubt a commonplace of thought. But such a use of conventional language does not affect St Paul's repudiation of body-versus-spirit dualism. We have to look elsewhere for the real significance of the conflict he describes.

Here is the issue. 'To live according to the flesh' is to live by the world's standards, by the lower impulses of unredeemed human nature, as if Christ had not died and risen again and bestowed his Spirit and as if we were not living within the new order. But 'to live according to the Spirit' is to live with the awareness of the new order into which we, as Christians, have been brought.

In Galatians 5 the contrast is between the works of the flesh and the harvest of the Spirit:

But I say, walk by the Spirit, and do not gratify the desires of the flesh. For the desires of the flesh are against the Spirit, and the desires of the Spirit are against the flesh; for these are opposed to each other, to prevent you from doing what you would. But if you are led by the Spirit you are not under the law. Now the works of the flesh are plain: immorality, impurity, licentiousness, idolatry, sorcery, enmity, strife, jealousy, anger, selfishness, dissension, party spirit, envy, drunkenness, carousing, and the like. I warn you, as I warned you before, that those who do such things shall not inherit the kingdom of God. But the fruit of the Spirit is love, joy, peace, patience, kindness, goodness, faithfulness, gentleness, self-control; against such there is no law. And those who belong to Christ Jesus have crucified the flesh with its passions and desires.

If we live by the Spirit, let us also walk by the Spirit. Let us have no self-conceit, no provoking of one another, no envy of one another (Gal. 5.16–26).

Thus does the apostle vividly contrast the old and the new.

The emphasis of this great passage is clear from the context. One danger for the Christians in Galatia is a reversion to a religion of law in place of the freedom of the gospel, and another danger is a kind of ethical libertarianism. 'The flesh' is the old unredeemed order, the lower nature. The sins which it prompts include indeed sins connected with the body – but also sins of selfish division and quarrelsomeness. The context strongly emphasizes the issues of love and brotherhood, for just before this passage St Paul has written 'through love be servants of one another' rather than 'bite and devour one another'. And the climax is the plea for humble, brotherly relations. The death to self which the Christian has died ('crucified the flesh with its passions and desires') is as much a death to divisive selfishness as to carnal lust. The harvest of the Spirit contains those gifts of character which belong to unselfish fellowship.

In Romans 8 the contrast is again between the rule of the Spirit on the one hand and the old religion of the law on the other. C. K. Barrett well paraphrases

verse 2, 'the religion (lit. the law) which is made possible in Christ Jesus, namely that of the life-giving
Spirit, liberating from the old religion (lit. law) which
is abused by sin and leads to death'. But the contrast
goes deeper, for 'the flesh' denotes man as living away
from God, away from the new world which Christ has
brought:

> For those who live according to the flesh set their
> minds on the things of the flesh, but those who live
> according to the Spirit set their minds on the things
> of the Spirit (Rom. 8.5).

I quote Barrett's comment:

> To have one's life determined by the flesh is not
> simply to have a corporeal existence (Christ himself
> did this) but to have one's gaze focused on all that
> flesh means and limited thereby to the world; to
> have one's mind set on existence apart from God.
> Correspondingly, to be determined by the Spirit is
> to have one's gaze focused upon that which cannot
> be seen, upon that invisible other which also gives
> meaning and authority to existence.[3]

The impasse is absolute, for the one way leads to death
and the other is life. Those who live according to the
flesh will die; those who put to death the deeds of the
body will live.

So St Paul's argument here leads on to sonship as the
outcome of life in the Spirit. 'All who are led by the
Spirit of God are sons of God' (Rom. 8.14). In Galatians the conflict of Spirit and flesh issues in the harvest of the Spirit, which is love and brotherhood. In
Romans the conflict leads on to the life of sonship.
Both characterize the new age.

THE COSMIC HOPE

The Christian life as St Paul sees it concerns not the human race alone, but the world of nature too. That world, in consequence of man's fall, is in deep frustration. Its deliverance will come when redeemed humanity reaches to the maturity of sonship, and then it too will be delivered into freedom and glory.

The picture in Romans 8 of the conflict between flesh and Spirit and of the sonship of the Christians, their suffering and glory, leads on to the picture of the cosmic frustration and the cosmic hope:

> I consider that the sufferings of this present time are not worth comparing with the glory that is to be revealed to us. For the creation waits with eager longing for the revealing of the sons of God; for the creation was subjected to futility, not of its own will but by the will of him who subjected it in hope; because the creation itself will be set free from its bondage to decay and obtain the glorious liberty of the children of God. We know that the whole creation has been groaning in travail together until now; and not only the creation, but we ourselves, who have the first fruits of the Spirit, groan inwardly as we wait for adoption as sons, the redemption of our bodies. For in this hope we were saved. Now hope that is seen is not hope. For who hopes for what he sees? But if we hope for what we do not see, we wait for it with patience (Rom. 8.18–25).

So the Christians share in the world's travail, but with hope in their hearts. The final freedom and glory belonging to their sonship is in store for them. When it comes, nature too will be freed.

The hope is kept alive in the Christians by their possession of the *arrabon* or 'first instalment' and the *aparche*, or first-fruits, of the Spirit. Already adopted as sons, they none the less await a future adoption; already sharers in Christ's resurrection they await the liberation of their bodies (cf. Rom. 8.11).

The Spirit helps us in our weakness; for we do not know how to pray as we ought, but the Spirit himself intercedes for us with sighs too deep for words. And he who searches the hearts of men knows what is the mind of the Spirit, because the Spirit intercedes for the saints according to the will of God (Rom. 8. 26–7).

St Paul may here be using a gnostic kind of description of the divine indwelling Spirit. But what he says about the Spirit's prayer is far distant from gnostic concepts. H. B. Swete's comment is still perhaps unsurpassed:

The very Spirit of God within us bears his part in our present difficulties. As he cries in us and we in him 'Abba, Father', so he shares the groans of our imperfect nature, converting them into prayers without and beyond words. There are times when we cannot pray in words, or pray as we ought; but our own inarticulate longings for a better life are the Spirit's intercessions on our behalf, audible to God who searches all hearts, and intelligible and acceptable to him since they are the voice of his Spirit, and it is according to his will that the Spirit should intercede for the members of his son.

There is perhaps nothing in the whole range of New Testament pneumatology which carries us so far into the heart of the Spirit's work. He is seen here in the most intimate relations with the human consciousness, distinct from it, yet associated with its imperfectly formed longings after righteousness, acting as an intercessor on its behalf in the sight of God, as the glorified Christ does; not however in heaven, but in the hearts of believers. The mystery of prayer stands here revealed, as far as it can be in this life; we see that it is the Holy Spirit who not only inspires the filial spirit which is the necessary condition of prayer, but is the author of the 'hearty desires' which are its essence.[3]

These searching words reach beyond the immediate context. The Spirit keeps alive in the Christians their hope of the world's deliverance, and of their own part in it. Thus they can share in the confident faith which St Paul goes on to describe in the climax of this great chapter. They can know that nothing lies outside God's omnipotence and love. They can know that 'in everything God works for good with those who love him', and they are those whom he has already glorified. So, come what may, the Christians are sure that they are 'more than conquerors through him who loved us' and that no circumstance or suffering, no power or phenomenon in any part of the universe, 'will be able to separate us from the love of God in Christ Jesus our Lord'.

Thus did the Christian experience of the Holy Spirit have its place in the new Christian apprehension of the sovereignty and fatherhood of God.

6

Spirit, Fellowship, Church

1

The line of division between the previous chapter and the present one is an arbitrary one and only the convenience of presenting the material can excuse the treatment of 'Spirit, Fellowship, Church' being separated from the treatment of 'the Spirit and the Christian life' – for essentially the themes are inseparable. All that was said in the previous chapter is misleading unless it is seen at every point in relation to 'fellowship'.

The word *koinonia*, which is usually translated 'fellowship' in the English versions, often means 'sharing together', whether of lives, interests, decisions, or property. So from the day of Pentecost the company of believers, enlarged by the accession of many new converts, were steadfast in the apostles' teaching, the fellowship, the breaking of the bread, and the prayers (Acts 2.42). No doubt the fellowship included their being together, sharing possessions in common (Acts 2.44), and being of 'one heart and soul'. The many-sided nature of *koinonia* is seen elsewhere in the apostolic writings. Thus the apostles in Jerusalem gave to Paul and Barnabas 'the right hand of fellowship' (Gal. 2.9), the Christians in Philippi had fellowship with Paul in the word of the gospel (Phil. 1.5), and the writer of the Epistle to the Hebrews urges his readers not to neglect to 'meet together' (Heb. 10.25).

But we also find *koinonia* meaning 'participation'. Here a deeper note is struck. St Paul tells the Christians in Corinth that they were called by God to participation in his Son (1 Cor. 1.9). He himself experiences participation in Christ's suffering (Phil. 3.10). The cup and the bread of the Eucharist are 'a participation in the blood of Christ ... a participation in the body of Christ' (1 Cor. 10.16). To be a Christian is indeed to have a life shared with the lives of one's fellows and with the life of Christ. None lives to himself and none dies to himself; and the self finds itself in and through other selves.[1] Such is the relation between Christ and Christians, and between Christians and God. Such is the experience and the belief which lies behind the phrase, 'the fellowship of the Holy Spirit'.

The phrase occurs but twice in the New Testament writings, in passages, however, of immense weight and importance. One is the blessing at the end of 2 Corinthians:

> The grace of the Lord Jesus Christ and the love of God and the fellowship of the Holy Spirit be with you all (2 Cor. 13.14).

The significance of this blessing speaks for itself. The other passage is St Paul's appeal to the Christians in Philippi to pursue true unity. He draws out the meaning of this unity on many levels of mind, heart, attitude, and action.

> So if there is any encouragement in Christ, any incentive of love, any participation in the Spirit, any affection and sympathy, complete my joy by being of the same mind, having the same love, being in full accord and of one mind. Do nothing from selfishness or conceit, but in humility count others better than yourselves. Let each of you look not only to his own interests, but to the interests of others. Have this

mind among yourselves, which you have in Christ
Jesus, who, though he was in the form of God, did
not count equality with God a thing to be grasped,
but emptied himself, taking the form of a servant
(Phil. 2.1–7).

This string of phrases is no repetitive rhetoric. Every
word tells, as the apostle draws out the meaning of
fellowship on its many levels. The fellowship has a
divine root, springing as it does from the incentive of
God's love, the mind of *Christ* and the fellowship of
the *Spirit*. The mind of Christ is defined as that of one
who sees his divine status as an opportunity not for
grasping but for pouring himself out and taking the
role of the servant. No phrase is more telling than 'the
mind which you have in Christ Jesus'. To act divinely
is not to grasp, but to pour self out; that is the secret of
the incarnation, and it is no less the secret of fellowship. Such indeed is the Christian way.

It has been questioned whether, in this passage, the
words 'if there is any *koinonia pneumatos*' mean 'if the
Spirit has created a fellowship' or 'if there is any participation in the Spirit'. Both senses, however, may be
implicit in the passage.

We turn now to St Paul's description of the Church
as the Body of Christ and the relation of that concept
to the Holy Spirit.

There has been much discussion of the background
of St Paul's language about the Body. The origin of
the language has been found in sources as diverse
as Stoicism, the Hebrew concept of corporate personality, and rabbinic speculations about the body of
Adam. It is one thing, however, to ask what linguistic
associations may have suggested the language to St

Paul and another thing to ask what events or experiences would cause him to seek such vocabulary at all. Here we can say without hesitation that the cause was the power of the risen Christ so working through the Holy Spirit as to mould the lives of the Christians into being the medium of his own activity, the 'body' of his risen life. The last Adam is the life-giving Spirit, and from him is derived the life in which the Christians are participants. The interweaving of language about the Church as the Body and language about the resurrection is noticeable (cf. 1 Cor. 6.19; Rom. 7.4–6, 8.11–12). To be united with the risen Christ is to be united with all who are his members.

There are two ways in which the imagery of the Body is used of the Church. In 1 Corinthians 12 Christ is the whole Body wherein the Christians are members.

> For just as the body is one and has many members, and all the members of the body, though many, are one body, so it is with Christ (1 Cor. 12.12).

In Ephesians,[2] however, Christ is the head over the Body which through the Spirit draws its life from him, completes him, and grows up into him. The risen Christ is Lord over all things 'for the church, which is his body, the fulness of him who fills all in all' (Eph. 1.22–3). It has been debated whether the word translated 'fulness', *pleroma*, should be translated 'that which Christ fills', or 'that by which Christ is completed', or 'that which is filled by him who is always being filled'.[3]

In the passage in 1 Corinthians the exposition of the Spirit and the Body comes in the context of disorders and problems concerning spiritual gifts and meetings of the Christian assembly in Corinth. Of this we shall say more presently. In Ephesians the exposition belongs to the writer's vision of the Church as the medium through which all mankind will be gathered into one. A drama of the role of the Spirit and the Body unfolds itself, reaching a climax in chapter 4. Here an exhortation to the readers to practise that fellowship which their calling demands leads on to:

There is one body and one Spirit, just as you were called to the one hope that belongs to your call, one Lord, one faith, one baptism, one God and Father of us all, who is above all and through all and in all (Eph. 4.4–6).

This in turn leads on to the account of the ascended Lord giving gifts to his Church:

And his gifts were that some should be apostles, some prophets, some evangelists, some pastors and teachers, for the equipment of the saints, for the work of ministry, for building up the body of Christ (Eph. 4.11–12).

We note that whereas in 1 Corinthians 12 the gifts are ascribed to the Spirit dividing as he will, they are here ascribed to the ascended Christ. If the former language emphasizes the place of gifts within the working of the one body, the latter language shows that the giving of the gifts is of the Lord's own will, purpose, and choice – a fact of supreme importance for the understanding of Christian vocation. We note also that the work of ministries is to equip *all* the saints for ministry in which all share. Then comes the goal:

... until we all attain to the unity of the faith and of the knowledge of the Son of God, to mature manhood, to the measure of the stature of the fulness of Christ (Eph. 4.13).

To this end the whole Body, through the working of every part, grows up into union with Christ the head. Practical counsel follows: 'Do not grieve the Holy Spirit of God' (Eph. 4.30). The personal language is here very marked. But the impersonal language continues: 'Do not get drunk with wine, for that is debauchery; but be filled with the Spirit' (5.18). Life in the Spirit is life 'always and for everything giving thanks in the name of our Lord Jesus Christ to God the Father' (5.20).

Besides the imagery of *fellowship* and of *body* there is the imagery of the spiritual *house* or *temple*.

Do you not know that you are God's temple and that God's Spirit dwells in you? If any one destroys God's temple, God will destroy him. For God's temple is holy, and that temple you are (1 Cor. 3.16–17).

... built upon the foundation of the apostles and prophets, Christ Jesus himself being the chief cornerstone, in whom the whole structure is joined together and grows into a holy temple in the Lord; in whom you also are built into it for a dwelling place of God in the Spirit (Eph. 2.20–2).

Come to him, to that living stone, rejected by men but in God's sight chosen and precious; and like living stones be yourselves built into a spiritual house (1 Pet. 2.4–5).

These passages show the imagery widespread, in the Petrine as well as the Pauline writings. And the relation of this imagery to the Holy Spirit is significant. In place of the temple of Solomon, made of stones and visited by the visible symbol of the 'glory of the Lord', there is now the temple composed of the lives of the Christians themselves and indwelt by the Holy Spirit.

The Christians are known not only by the images of fellowship, body, and temple but by being themselves, in no image but literally, the *people of God*. They are the new Israel, whose status is derived not from physical race but from the call of God and the brotherhood of the new covenant. Such is the meaning of the word *ecclesia*. The local community of Christians in any place is the one people of God as represented in that place. This aspect is powerfully brought out by St Paul in the opening greeting of 1 Corinthians:

> To the church of God which is at Corinth, to those sanctified in Christ Jesus, called to be saints together with all those who in every place call on the name of our Lord Jesus Christ, both their Lord and ours (1 Cor. 1.2).

The same concept appears, without the use of the word *ecclesia*, in the First Epistle of St Peter:

> But you are a chosen race, a royal priesthood, a holy nation, God's own people (1 Pet. 2.9).

Two corollaries of this language are apparent. One is that the unity of Christians is basically that of a common spiritual birth and brotherhood. The other is that they are, like Israel, distinguished in the world by the call to holiness into a holy God, but now with the new depth involved in their possession of the Holy Spirit. Fellowship, body, temple, people of God: in each of these concepts the Holy Spirit is the determining factor.

2

We return now to the question of 'spiritual gifts' which agitated the church of Corinth.

'Now concerning spiritual gifts': in these words St Paul begins a discussion (1 Cor. 12–14) which has through the centuries been of supreme practical and theological importance for Christians. But the context is a specific one, for while he says things about spiritual gifts which concern the whole life of the Church, he is dealing specially with the problems of behaviour in the Corinthian assembly. Therein was much excited behaviour, including both ecstatic prayers and blasphemous utterances. St Paul writes at the outset that blasphemies cannot issue from the Holy Spirit, and only the Holy Spirit enables a person to say 'Jesus is Lord'. But through the three chapters (12, 13, and 14) the references to 'speaking in tongues' show that it was a paramount problem. This was a kind of 'hyper-enthusiastic vocalization which was quite unintelligible except to a chosen few',[4] but to those who engaged in it it was full of significance as a release of the personality in wordless and joyful praise of God. No doubt this gift was prominent in the Gentile churches, and in the Acts of the Apostles there are instances of this gift being regarded as evidence of the presence of the Holy Spirit in those who had been converted.

To this exciting situation, fraught with the danger

of division through jealousies about gifts and their use,
St Paul responds by his teaching about the One Body,
by his appeal to love in the Hymn of Love and by some
incisive practical counsels.

The Spirit gives varieties of gifts, *charismata*, which
are not personal qualities or possessions so much as
actions of the divine *charis* or grace in direct impact
upon the persons concerned.[5] These gifts include: the
utterance of wisdom, the utterance of knowledge,
faith, healing, miracles, prophecy, the distinguishing
of spirits, various kinds of tongues, the interpretation
of tongues. All these gifts come from the one and same
Spirit who distributes them as he wills. But to understand their relationship it is necessary to remember the
essential nature of the Church:

> For just as the body is one and has many members,
> and all the members of the body, though many, are
> one body, so it is with Christ. For by one Spirit we
> were all baptized into one body – Jews or Greeks,
> slaves or free – and all were made to think of one
> Spirit (1 Cor. 12.12–13).

Then follows the account of the mutual dependence of
the members upon one another, enjoying their diversity for the sake of the whole. And the imagery passes
beyond that of limbs into that of persons, for 'if one
member suffers, all suffer together; if one member is
honoured, all the members rejoice'. And, in a further
plea for mutual esteem, St Paul goes on to speak of the
offices or functions which the Spirit bestows: apostles,
prophets, teachers, workers of miracles, healers, helpers,
administrators, speakers in tongues. Not every member of the Church can or should perform all these

roles. So what is it that every member of the Church must do? Let him 'earnestly desire [be ambitious for] the higher gifts, and I will show you a still more excellent way'. It is the way of love, and St Paul moves on to the words of the Hymn of Love.

The Hymn of Love breaks with prophetic beauty upon the scene of controversy and disorder. Love is not one of the *charismata*, it is for all Christians and without it all the *charismata* are futile. Tongues, prophecy, faith, renunciation, martyrdom, all are vain. 'Faith, hope, love abide, these three; but the greatest of these is love' (1 Cor. 13.13).

The Hymn ended, practical counsels follow. St Paul turns closely to the happenings in the Christian assemblies. He has *glossolalia* specially in mind, as it comes at the beginning of the Hymn of Love and comes now at the beginning of his counsels. 'Make love your aim; and earnestly desire the spiritual gifts, especially that you may prophesy' (1 Cor. 14.1). To speak in tongues is a genuine gift, St Paul himself possesses it; it is the voice of sincere prayer to God. But it does not edify the assembly unless there are present those able to interpret it, whereas prophecy does edify. When St Paul says, 'Tongues are a sign not for believers but for unbelievers, while prophecy is not for unbelievers but for believers' (14.22), he may mean that, whereas tongues could be evidence to the convert from outside the Church that the Spirit had been given to him, inside the Church tongues had no such evidential value. On the other hand prophecy could be unmeaning to those outside, but was full of value within the Church.[6] Throughout the discussion St Paul's high regard for prophecy is again and again apparent. So we reach the climax:

So, my brethren, earnestly desire to prophesy, and do not forbid speaking in tongues (1 Cor. 14.39).

Prophecy is the power to discern the will and purpose of God and to declare it; a Church that lives after the Spirit will have this gift diffused among its members; it will be a prophetic Church; it will be a Church sometimes able to say with conviction, 'It has seemed good to the Holy Spirit and to us' (Acts 15.28).

There are limits to the extent to which we can draw from St Paul's discussion of the Spirit and the gifts, counsels or principles applicable to all times and contexts. But clearly the doctrines of love and of members in the Body stand for all time, as well as the primacy of prophecy in the life of the Church. Otherwise we learn the wrongness of exalting any one gift into a special mark of spirituality. As to *glossolalia*, it is clearly not a sign of spiritual excellence, but it would be unfair to conclude from St Paul's warnings about its small value *in the assemblies* that he would belittle its place in the Christian life as a liberation of a Christian into a joyful outburst of praise. Such may have been its significance at Pentecost and at some of the occasions of the reception of the Spirit by converts. But *spiritus ubi vult spirat*, and St Paul is telling the Corinthians, to help us for all time, how many are his gifts.

3

The Church exists by the power of the Holy Spirit. Whether as fellowship, or body, or temple, or people of God, it has no existence apart from the impact of the Holy Spirit upon human lives. Inasmuch as the Spirit is derived from Jesus Christ who died and rose again, the Church is called to bear continual witness to the history in which the gospel of God is embodied.

The converts were initiated into the Church, in any and every place, by the rite of baptism. This rite, administered by the plunging of the candidate into water, involved profession of faith in Jesus as Lord, reception of the Holy Spirit, incorporation into the Body of Christ, and a death to self which was an act of identification with Christ's death, issuing in a new life which was a participation in Christ's risen life. While the rite united the converts with the contemporary Christ through the contemporary Spirit within the contemporary Christian fellowship, it was an act of commitment to the death of Christ once died.

The Eucharist was the centre of the Church's common life. In this rite the Christians shared in the contemporary life of Christ in fellowship with one another. But this life was the life which had once died, the life defined by the broken body and sacrificial blood. The feeding on the life was possible because in the rite there was the *anamnesis* or recalling of the death. The rite was thus a proclamation of the continuing significance of the saving gospel history.

What is true of baptism and the Eucharist is true of the Christians' life in the Spirit. It is a life guided by the Spirit's continuing promptings in contemporary situations, and a life of growth and movement towards future realizations of the Spirit's power. Thus the Spirit leads the Christians towards the full apprehension of that to which they were once for all committed. St Paul, counting himself not yet to have apprehended, presses on, 'that I may know him and the power of his resurrection, and may share his sufferings, becoming like him in his death' (Phil. 3.10). Life in the Spirit is a life of new adventures and discoveries while being a life of continuing witness to the history whereby it has been created.

It is this historical character of Christianity which gives to the Church not only the mission of the Spirit but certain media of continuity through which the Spirit acts in the Church's common life: these media of continuity include the sacraments, the apostolic ministry, and a tradition of teaching. The Church is thus not without visible shape, and this shape is itself a witness to the history of salvation. But while the Spirit uses this shape and the media which constitute it, the Spirit also acts in unpredictable ways, exposing, teaching, illuminating, judging, renewing. The Spirit is still the unpredictable *ruach* of God.

The tension between these two aspects of the Spirit's action has been apparent again and again in the Christian centuries from the apostolic age onwards. There have been times when the Spirit's appeal to tradition has enabled a true answer to be made to tendencies which might tear Christianity from the historic gospel. There have also been times when the appeal to tradition has caused a kind of fossilized traditionalism which while asserting the Creed can fail to witness that Christ is risen; the tensions between what have been called the 'horizontal' and the 'vertical' aspects of the life of the Spirit have occurred in many forms, sometimes leading to deep cleavage between an 'institutitional' and a 'charismatic' Christianity. What light does our study of the Holy Spirit in the apostolic age throw upon this problem?

It seems that there are three considerations which may be always helpful for our wrestling with this problem. First, the linguistic uses in the Bible are still relevant to our understanding of the ways of the Spirit. We found in our biblical study language about Spirit as an indwelling possession with the imagery of a kind of fluid or substance within people. We found also Spirit as the violent, unpredictable invasion of persons and institutions from without, disturbing, frightening, exalting. Both these uses are relevant for our ecclesiology.

Second, it is a mistake in ecclesiology to dwell exclusively upon one of the images of the Church and to press its implications with a rigid kind of logic. Sometimes, in ecumenical circles, this has been done with the imagery of the Church as the Body. More edifying is it to ring the changes often between the varieties of ecclesiological imagery – the fellowship, the body, the temple, the people – and to be confined to none. So there can be a more lively understanding of the Spirit and the Church.

Third, the study of the New Testament demands that we should always have in mind the eschatological or futuristic aspect of the Church. The Church is already given, once for all created, nevertheless it does not yet appear what the Church shall be. It anticipates in hope the life of the age to come.

We have seen how basic is the eschatological aspect of the Spirit, as the promise and the first-fruits of the coming age. As is the Spirit, so is the Church. Its characteristics are once for all given, and it grows in their realization. Ephesians 4 depicts the Church as growing to the measure of the stature of the fulness of Christ, and this picture is applicable to each of the 'notes' of the Church. Possessing unity, the Church grows in the working-out of its meaning through many phases of history and cultural contexts, and the story of the church of Corinth is an epitome of the long Christian centuries. Possessing holiness in the call of God and in the Spirit of holiness, the Church grows along the way of Christ's holiness. Possessing truth, for Christ himself is the truth, the Church will grow in the apprehension of the truth which is Christ. In each of these ways the Church's God-given authority is realized in the Church's humble recognition of the 'not yet'. Thus is the Church discouraged from making absolute its present apprehension of unity, or truth, or holiness. Yet in each of these spheres the Church's ability to learn and to grow is rooted in its continuing witness to Jesus Christ.

We shall ask in the next two chapters how this aspect of the work of the Holy Spirit is illuminated in the Gospel of St John.

7

St John: Spirit and Glory

1

The teaching of the Fourth Gospel concerning the
Holy Spirit has behind it not only the theological in-
sight of its author and the traditions on which he
draws, but also the Church's continuous experience of
the Holy Spirit in the apostolic age. Without the experience it is doubtful whether such a book could ever
have been written, as it presupposes a Christianity
which is lively, creative, and able to move fearlessly
into new cultural environments. The conflict between
the Church and the world had been happening
wherever the gospel had spread; and, though the word
'Paraclete' may never have been used in earlier Christian writings, the tasks assigned to the Paraclete of
witnessing to Christ, convicting the world, comforting
the disciples, and glorifying Christ, were part of the
history of the apostolic age. The Fourth Evangelist is
not only expounding a particular theology for the
needs of a particular situation; he is witnessing to
experience and to ideas already apparent in the
Church.

None the less, the Fourth Gospel has its own context, purpose, and standpoint, for it was written to
meet the needs of a specific Christian community.
While there have always been those who have argued
for the Jewish associations of this Gospel, the main
trend of scholarship has been towards an emphasis
upon its Greek environment. That environment was
at least in part a gnostic kind of religion. Thus there is

the contrast between the realm of spirit and the realm of flesh, the realm of light and the realm of darkness. There is the quest for knowledge. There is the 'myth' of the saviour who descends from the realm of spirit into the world and, after conquering the evil one, returns whence he came. But, as with St Paul, so with the Fourth Evangelist, the differences from gnosticism are profound. No one has brought this out more strongly than Rudolf Bultmann, who, after describing the gnostic affinities of the Fourth Gospel, goes on to say of the author:

> In his gnostic form a pointed anti-gnosticism is expressed. John knows no gnostic dualism. Therefore in John man is not seen dualistically. Flesh and Spirit do not stand opposed as substances of the demonic and divine realms. Rather it is stressed, with all sharpness, that the Redeemer has become *flesh* and shows his glory precisely as the one made flesh. Man's lostness in the world is not the lost condition of a heavenly substance in the power of darkness, but the sinful turning away of the creature from the Creator. In place of cosmic dualism steps a dualism of decision; life and death are not determined for all time on natural grounds, but depend on the decision of faith and of unbelief.[1]

To come to God, to know the truth, to receive the Spirit, to pass from darkness to light, depends not upon deliverance from the flesh into a spirit realm, but upon the historical mission of Jesus the Messiah who lived and died in the flesh. True, it is fatal to trust in the flesh, or to regard the flesh as sufficient, for 'nature' cannot redeem itself, and it is by the power of the Spirit that deliverance comes. The Spirit alone gives life. But the action of the Spirit is derived from the mission of Jesus in history; and history matters supremely to the Fourth Evangelist, ready as he is to interpret its meaning rather than to narrate it as a chronicler.

The theme of the Holy Spirit in the Fourth Gospel is drawn out in three phases. First, there is the Holy Spirit in the mission and teaching of Jesus in Galilee and Judaea. Second, there is the teaching in the last discourse at the supper. Third, there are the references to the gift of the Holy Spirit in the narratives of the passion and the resurrection.

2

St John (as we will call the author without prejudging his identity) does not describe the baptism of Jesus. But he tells how the Baptist testifies that Jesus is the one upon whom the Spirit descends and the one who will in turn bestow the Spirit:

And John bore witness, 'I saw the Spirit descend as a dove from heaven, and it remained on him. I myself did not know him; but he who sent me to baptize with water said to me, "He on whom you see the Spirit descend and remain, this is he who baptizes with the Holy Spirit." And I have seen and have borne witness that this is the Son of God' (John 1.32-4).

So, endowed with the Holy Spirit, Jesus pursues his mission; and whereas in the synoptists his theme is the kingdom of God, his theme in John is life, light, glory. Meanwhile there is in John, as in the synoptists, reticence about the Spirit in the teaching of Jesus. Indeed there are only three significant occasions of teaching before we come in chapter 7 to the episode which can be called the 'crunch'. These episodes are (1) the private dialogue with Nicodemus in chapter 3; (2) the private dialogue with the woman of Samaria in chapter 4; (3) the reference to the Spirit at the end of the teaching on the Bread of Life in chapter 6.

1   Nicodemus, a Pharisee, comes to Jesus by night. Perhaps he is attracted by what he knows of Jesus, and wants to express appreciation and the desire to know more, and to combine new knowledge with what he knows already. But the reply of Jesus cuts right across Nicodemus' approach. A new order is here, calling for rebirth, and without rebirth a man cannot enter the kingdom of God. Nicodemus is smitten with incredulity, and Jesus continues the theme; without rebirth by 'water and spirit' a man cannot even *see* the kingdom of God. The mention of water no doubt relates the teaching to the sacrament of baptism; but the emphasis is upon the character of the rebirth by the power of the Spirit, as mighty and mysterious as a gale of wind:

> Truly, truly, I say to you, unless one is born of water and the Spirit, he cannot enter the kingdom of God. That which is born of the flesh is flesh, and that which is born of the Spirit is spirit. Do not marvel that I said to you, 'You must be born anew. The wind blows where it wills, and you hear the sound of it, but you do not know whence it comes or whither it goes; so it is with every one who is born of the Spirit' (3.5–8).

Still incredulous, Nicodemus is told that, wonderful though these things are, they are 'earthly'; they belong to the rudiments, in contrast with the 'heavenly things' which will follow. To these Nicodemus is finally directed – and what are they?

> And as Moses lifted up the serpent in the wilderness, so must the Son of man be lifted up, that whoever believes in him may have eternal life (3.14–15).

The gift to the believer of eternal life, which is no doubt equivalent to entrance into the kingdom of God, will turn upon the crucifixion of Jesus. Nicodemus came to witness this. Few things are more moving in the narrative of this Gospel than the reappearance of Nicodemus to assist in the burial of Jesus:

> Nicodemus also, who had at first come to him by night, came bringing a mixture of myrrh and aloes, about a hundred pounds' weight (John 19.39).

So he begins to see the Kingdom of God!

2   The second episode concerning the Spirit is also in private. Jesus is in Samaria, by Jacob's well at Sychar, and being thirsty he asks a strange, local woman to give him a drink. She is astonished at being spoken to in this way by a Jew, for Jews and Samaritans are deeply estranged. But Jesus moves into another plane and says:

> If you knew the gift of God, and who it is that is saying to you, 'Give me a drink', you would have asked him, and he would have given you living water (4.10).

Bewildered, the woman continues the talk on the original plane; but Jesus continues:

> Every one who drinks of this water will thirst again, but whoever drinks of the water that I shall give him will never thirst; the water that I shall give him will become in him a spring of water welling up to eternal life (4.13–14).

The woman longs for this water; but her thoughts are still on the natural plane. But Jesus was speaking to her about the Spirit, and the Spirit is the *arrabon* of eternal life.

As with St Paul and the earlier traditions, here too the eschatological note sounds throughout the doctrine of Spirit. But whereas in the earlier traditions Spirit is the foretaste of the future glory when the Lord returns, in John Spirit is the pointer to the eternal life available when once the Son of man has been glorified.

The conversation continues. When the woman finds that Jesus knows she has had five husbands and is now living in sin, she is sure he is a prophet. In her embarrassment she turns the talk from her own past to familiar ecclesiastical controversy: whether Mount Zion (the Jews) or Mount Gerizim (the Samaritans) is the right place for the worship of God. Jesus picks this up, and speaks of the new order:

> Woman, believe me, the hour is coming when neither on this mountain nor in Jerusalem will you worship the Father. You worship what you do not know; we worship what we know, for salvation is from the Jews. But the hour is coming, and now is, when the true worshippers will worship the Father

in spirit and truth, for such the Father seeks to worship him. God is spirit, and those who worship him
must worship in spirit and truth (4.21–4).

As not seldom in the gospel tradition the new order is
both here and to come; the double stance, however,
finds special vividness in the phrase which recurs in
this Gospel: 'The hour is coming, and now is' (cf. 4.23;
5.25; 16.32). And the hour brings a worship in which
neither Zion nor Gerizim will have a special place, because it will be worship 'in spirit and truth'. And this,
because God is Spirit.

That God is Spirit is a notion which is found both
in the Old Testament and in Hellenistic religion. He
is immaterial, in contrast with all visible objects; but
in the Old Testament there is the further thought of
his power as creator and ruler of the world. Truth is
also a Hellenistic concept, but no less a biblical one,
for Yahweh is the God of truth. More important, however, than both the Greek and the biblical background
is the Johannine teaching that Jesus is himself the
truth as well as the way and the life; and the Paraclete
whom he sends is named the Spirit of Truth (John
14.6, 15.26). Worship in the new order brought by the
Messiah will be worship freed from the domination of
particular sites and buildings, not because of an anti-
material 'inwardness' but because the new order belongs to God who is Spirit and to Jesus who is truth.

3   The third dialogue about Spirit comes at the end
of the discourse on the Bread of Life. Here Jesus is in
dialogue not with an individual person, but with a
number of hearers, first bewildered Jews and then no
less bewildered disciples.

The exposition of the Bread of Life has tried the hearers of Jesus very high. First, he speaks of the true Bread, then he identifies himself with this Bread, and finally he defines the Bread as his flesh, to be given 'for the life of the world'. The Jews react with horror, and ask, 'How can this man give us his flesh to eat?' And Jesus goes further and says that the man who would receive eternal life must eat his flesh and drink his blood. Many of the disciples murmur and in answer to their murmuring Jesus says:

> Do you take offence at this? Then what if you were to see the Son of man ascending where he was before? It is the spirit that gives life, the flesh is of no avail; the words that I have spoken to you are spirit and life (6.61–3).

These words disclose the heart of Johannine doctrine. Is the eating of the flesh of the Son of man an incredible idea? Something as startling is to happen – the ascension of the Son of man to heaven where he was before. But these happenings, both the feeding upon Christ and the ascension of Christ to heaven, belong to the life-giving Spirit and without the Spirit they are nothing. The words of Jesus are Spirit and life; they are filled with the power of the Spirit and they are life-giving in effect.

What is here said seems to apply both to the mission of the Christ and to the Eucharistic gift. Both involve flesh, the flesh of history and the flesh of material food. Both are nothing without the Spirit's power.

3

In each of the three dialogues about the Spirit there has been a looking forward, an eschatological note; now we pass on to the episode where the clue is found.

Jesus is in Jerusalem at the time of the Feast of Tabernacles, the feast which included the pouring of water on the temple steps while the words were recited: 'With joy you will draw water from the wells of salvation' (Isa. 12.3). Jesus uses the occasion for some prophetic words:

> On the last day of the feast, the great day, Jesus stood up and proclaimed, 'If any one thirst, let him come to me and let him who believes in me drink.[2] As the scripture has said, "Out of his heart shall flow rivers of living water." ' Now this he said about the Spirit, which those who believed in him were to receive; for as yet the Spirit had not yet been given, because Jesus was not yet glorified (John 7.37–9).

The word 'given' has no equivalent in the Greek text, which is '*pneuma*, spirit not yet'. But 'given' is obviously to be understood. In this one sentence we have the key to the Johannine doctrine. Jesus is predicting the gift of the Spirit to the believer, but first he must be glorified by his death on the cross. Death, glory, Spirit: that is the sequence.

That the Spirit is primarily the gift of Jesus crucified and risen has been familiar in the earlier traditions. It is this theme which the Fourth Gospel draws out in the concept of glory.

Glory is a keynote of the Fourth Gospel. God's glory is his splendour, majesty, character, power. 'The Word became flesh and dwelt among us ... we have beheld his glory' (1.14). The divine glory is shown forth in the birth and mission of Jesus, and the narrative of the Gospel traces its manifestation in the signs which he performs and the teaching which he gives. But as the story proceeds, a strange elusiveness about the glory appears. Jesus does not glorify himself, he does not have a glory of his own, he glorifies the Father, and in turn the Father glorifies him:

> If I glorify myself, my glory is nothing; it is my Father who glorifies me (8.54).

> He who speaks on his own authority seeks his own glory; but he who seeks the glory of him who sent him is true, and in him there is no falsehood (7.18).

For the glory which Jesus reveals is the eternal glory of self-giving love wherein the Father glorifies the Son and the Son glorifies the Father: it is this glory which is being disclosed in the mission of Jesus in history.

There is thus a sharp contrast and conflict between divine glory as Jesus discloses it, and human glory as man understands it. Indeed the contrast is a linguistic one, for in ancient secular Greek the word *doxa* meant a man's personal distinction or status, or the honour which others give to him; whereas in biblical Greek it meant the divine power and splendour – now identified in the Fourth Gospel with divine self-giving love. In a single poignant sentence Jesus is recorded as diagnosing the conflict:

> How can you believe, who receive glory from one another and do not seek the glory that comes from the only God? (5.44).

These are piercing words. The people did not believe, for they were so preoccupied with the false glory of status and the dignity which men seek for themselves and ascribe to one another, that they did not recognize or desire the true glory which Jesus was bringing to them. The irreconcilable conflict is exposed.

The conflict between divine glory in Jesus and false glory in man leads on to the passion. In their concern to preserve national and ecclesiastical status undisturbed, the chief priests plot the destruction of Jesus. But in the events which culminate in the crucifixion the divine glory shines. The hour comes when the Son of man is glorified.

So the bestowal of the Spirit upon the believers is now possible. If the manifestation of divine glory in Jesus is the first chapter, the second chapter is the giving of the glory to the disciples (cf. 17.22). This is the work of the Holy Spirit: a work whose many aspects are drawn out in the discourse at the supper and whose deepest meaning is seen in the sentence, 'He shall glorify me' (16.14).

As Jesus glorified the Father in his mission on earth, so the Spirit will glorify Jesus in the lives of those who believe.

8

St John: The Paraclete

The discourse at the supper dwells upon the departure of the Lord from the disciples and their new relationship with him which will follow. In the intensity of their present union with him they dread the thought of being without him. Yet his departure is necessary for them, for by clinging to his visible presence they would miss the deeper relationship to which he desires to lead them and the deeper knowledge of him and of the Father.

Hitherto the relation of the Lord to the disciples had been circumscribed by the conditions of his earthly life; and in Hort's words, 'As yet it was hardly possible for them to feel the difference between his being with them where they were and their being with him where he was ... that was the transition now coming, the transition from a presence taking its character from their circumstances to a presence taking its character from his.'[1] It is this new relation which the discourse describes; it will be a return of the Lord to them but in such a manner that to say that they go to him will be as true as to say he comes to them.

Within the discourse there are four passages about the Holy Spirit. It is well first to identify these in their contexts and to see how they are related to the discourse, whether as interruptions or as illuminating the theme.

1   If you love me, you will keep my commandments.

And I will pray the Father, and he will give you another Paraclete, to be with you for ever, even the Spirit of truth, whom the world cannot receive, because it neither sees him nor knows him; you know him, for he dwells with you, and will be in you (14.15–17).

2 These things I have spoken to you, while I am still with you. But the Paraclete, the Holy Spirit, whom the Father will send in my name, he will teach you all things, and bring to your remembrance all that I have said to you (14.25–6).

3 (Now they have seen and hated both me and my Father.) But when the Paraclete comes ... even the Spirit of truth, who proceeds from the Father, he will bear witness to me; and you also are witnesses, because you have been with me from the beginning (15.26–7).

4 Nevertheless I tell you the truth: it is to your advantage that I go away, for if I do not go away, the Paraclete will not come to you; but if I go, I will send him to you. And when he comes, he will convince the world of sin and of righteousness and of judgment: of sin, because they do not believe in me; of righteousness, because I go to the Father, and you will see me no more; of judgment, because the ruler of this world is judged.

I have yet many things to say to you, but you cannot bear them now. When the Spirit of truth comes, he will guide you into all the truth; for he will not speak on his own authority, but whatever he hears he will speak, and he will declare to you the things that are to come. He will glorify me, for he will take what is mine and declare it to you. All that the

Father has is mine; therefore I said that he will take what is mine and declare it to you (16.7–14).

The R.S.V. has here been followed except that the word *Paraclete* is used, instead of the R.S.V. translation, 'Counsellor', for we have yet to consider how the Greek word *parakletos* should be translated and understood.

Do the four passages about the Holy Spirit 'interrupt' the flow of the discourse? In a sense they may seem to do so, for the theme of the discourse is the Lord's own return to the disciples. Yet the double strain introduced by the references to the Spirit need not surprise us when we have already learned from St Paul and others, how close are the Spirit and the risen Christ. The implication of the discourse is that the sending of the Paraclete is the means whereby the Lord himself returns to the disciples, to the glory of the Father. Receiving the Spirit's ministrations the disciples will know of Christ's own presence with them. Yet, for all the affinity of the Spirit to Christ, the Spirit is distinct and personal; the emphatic personal pronoun following the neuter noun (*to pneuma-ekeinos*), vividly shows this. It is Christ who will send the Spirit, from the Father (15.26; 16.7), and it is also the Father who will send the Spirit in answer to the prayer of Christ (14.16).

From the four passages about the Spirit, we may summarize his mission thus:

1 The Spirit will indwell the disciples (14.17).
2 He will teach (14.26) and he is the Spirit of truth (14.17; 16.13).
3 He will recall to the disciples what Jesus said to them (14.26).

4 He will witness to Christ, and enable the disciples to witness (15.26).
5 He will convict the world (16.8–11).
6 He will declare to the disciples the things that are coming, and he will glorify Christ by taking the things that are Christ's and declaring them to the disciples (16.13–14).

Such will be the work of the Spirit. He will teach, witness, convince, guide into truth, and declare what is to come; and every part of this ministry is derived from, and in turn points to, the historic mission and teaching of Jesus.

2

Four times the Spirit is named as the Paraclete, and in the first of these instances he is called 'another Paraclete'. Jesus, it is implied, has been the first Paraclete; now, with the departure of Jesus, the second Paraclete will be sent. We need to ask what the word means, and how it is related to the functions which the discourse describes.[2]

The usual meaning of *parakletos* outside the New Testament is 'one called to help' – the pleader, the legal assistant, the advocate in a court of law. There is much in the discourse which suggests this sense; the work of the Paraclete includes convicting the world, and witnessing to the truth. But it is also relevant that the verb *parakalein* and the noun *paraklesis* are used of Christians preaching (cf. Acts 2.40), and this may give to the word Paraclete a nuance reaching beyond the legal sense. So, too, in the Greek Bible, both the verb and the noun are used of the divine consolation expected in the messianic age, and this justifies the rendering 'Comforter'. It is, then, both as Advocate and as Comforter that the Spirit will aid the disciples.

1 We turn to the work of the Spirit as Advocate. The atmosphere of a trial is prominent in the Fourth Gospel. There is the trial of Jesus before the High Priest and before Pilate, and if they are ostensibly the judges they are in a deep sense the defendants in Jesus' arrangement of the world in the name of truth. Throughout the Gospel the conflict between Jesus and the world is a conflict between truth and falsehood, and a series of witnesses are invoked: the baptist, the scriptures, the words of Jesus, the Father, the works of Jesus, Jesus himself, an unnamed disciple. Witness has of course a meaning by no means confined to the law court, and the forensic image may not be present throughout. But it is hard to doubt its presence in the passage in chapter 16 about the conviction of the world.

Few words in the Gospel are more haunting than these:

> And when he comes, he will convince the world concerning sin and righteousness and judgment: concerning sin, because they do not believe in me; concerning righteousness, because I go to the Father, and you will see me no more; concerning judgment, because the ruler of this world is judged (16.8–11).

The exact meaning of these sentences turns upon the way we render the preposition *peri* and the particle *hoti*. Does the writer mean conviction 'concerning', 'in respect of' sin, righteousness, and judgement; or does he mean conviction 'of' sin, righteousness, and judgement? Again, is the conviction 'in that they do not believe in me', etc. or is it 'because they do not believe in me'? It has been perhaps the most familiar interpretation to paraphrase thus: 'He will convict the world in regard to sin, showing that sin consists in not believing in me; in regard to righteousness, showing that righteousness consists in my departure to the Father; in regard to judgement, showing that in the passion it is the prince of the world who is judged.' Thus the Spirit works in the conscience of the world to bring about the reversal of its errors on these three stupendous themes. Where the world believed itself to be judging, it will find itself judged and its errors exposed. This interpretation is indeed in line with the tenor of the Fourth Gospel as a whole.

The difficulty, however, felt about this interpretation is that in John 8.46 the word *peri* plainly means 'of': 'Which of you convicts me *of* sin?'[3] If that meaning is followed in the passage we are discussing then the Spirit will convict the world *of* its sin, *of* the righteousness of Christ, and *of* the judgement of the ruler of the world. Whichever interpretation is followed, it will be the Spirit's work to stir the world's conscience and to confute its errors. But a further question is this. Does the conviction of the world mean only that its guilt is demonstrated as in a court, or does it mean also that there comes about conviction in the sense of a change of attitudes? In a word, is the outcome confrontation only or is it conversion too? The latter is, I would myself suggest, in line with John 12.31–2: 'Now is the judgment of this world, now shall the ruler of this world be cast out; and I, when I am lifted up from the earth, will draw all men to myself.' Here the impact of the crisis is indeed a confrontation, but it issues in the drawing of mankind to

Christ which means also conversion. For all the inevitability of judgement, Christ came not to judge but to save.

2 The Spirit is also the *Comforter*. Already our discussion has moved beyond what the legal imagery is able to express. It is in the strictly biblical sense of comfort that the Paraclete has this role. The prophets and the psalmists had sometimes spoken of the coming of the divine comfort to Israel, and it was for the divine comfort that the aged Simeon was waiting when he welcomed the infant Jesus in the temple (Luke 2.25). The divine comfort included the bringing of peace and prosperity to the people, with good crops and harvests, and corn and wine and oil in plenty. But it included also the extirpation of crime and injustice in the land and the establishment of God's righteous will with repentance as its condition; in a word, the whole blessing of messianic salvation. Such is the comfort which the Paraclete will bring to the disciples with a new inwardness and intimacy. They will have both peace and joy, the peace of which Jesus speaks as being not of this world (14.27) and the joy which is his own (15.11). This comfort will be in the face of tribulation (16.38), and it will be inseparable from the Spirit's conviction. In the words of E. C. Hoskyns, 'The consolation of the disciples is consolation in the face of condemnation and if *Comforter* secures recognition of God's boundless mercy, *Advocate* secures recognition of the sternness of the issue.'

Both aspects of the Paraclete will be in mind when we pass on to the last words about the Spirit in the discourse, words replete with the themes of truth, judgement, and glory:

I have yet many things to say to you, but you cannot bear them now. When the Spirit of truth comes, he will guide you into all the truth; for he will not speak on his own authority, but whatever he hears he will speak, and he will declare to you the things that are to come. He will glorify me, for he will take what is mine and declare it to you. All that the Father has is mine; therefore I said that he will take what is mine and declare it to you (16.12–15).

The Spirit in his mission will depend upon Christ and hearken to Christ, as Christ depends upon the Father and hearkens to the Father. As teacher of the disciples he will be continuing the teaching which Christ had begun. He will guide them along the road into the fulness of that truth which is Jesus himself (14.6). The 'things that are to come', which the Spirit will declare, means probably the things imminently coming in the setting of the supper – the crucifixion and the resurrection of Jesus; and it is these events which are the key to the truth which is Jesus. In this way the Spirit will 'glorify' Christ, taking the things of Christ ('what is mine', *ta ema*) and proclaiming them. As Christ glorified the Father by declaring the things of the Father, so the Spirit will glorify Christ by declaring the things of Christ in the lives of the disciples.

May we not see the Spirit's work of teaching and interpreting apparent within the history of the apostolic age? The understanding of the relation of Christ to the disciples, to God, and to the world in the developing phases of the New Testament writings would seem to illustrate this part of the Spirit's mission; and no example of this is more significant than the Fourth Gospel itself. Nor need we think of this work of the

Spirit in the interpretation of Christ as confined to the apostolic age. But it is always into the truth of *Christ* that the Spirit leads the Church, and Christ is for ever the divine Son who lived, died, and rose again. It is as the disciples witness to what Christ taught, and recall his words, that the Spirit's mission of truth is fulfilled.

3

So it is that in all that he does the Spirit glorifies Christ in the disciples. The discourse dwells upon the Spirit's relation both to the Father and to Christ. Whereas St Paul links the Spirit with the Father in some contexts and with the risen Christ in other contexts, the last discourse in John links the Spirit with both within the same passages. We shall in the final chapter be asking what are the implications of this for the Christian doctrine of God. Here we notice only that at the heart of St John's understanding of the eternal glory of the Father and the Son there is the revelation of this glory in the self-giving love of the passion. When the Spirit guides the believers into the truth they will know that 'what is mine' and 'the things that are to come' are the key. From the supper Jesus and the disciples go on across the Kidron valley to the garden, and 'the things that are to come' begin. At intervals in the story there have been haunting references to the time when the glory will be complete: the lifting-up of the Son of man, the glorifying, the going to the Father, the hour, the day, pointing to a climax yet to come. When Jesus dies, 'that hour' has come (19.27) and the day of the resurrection is 'that day' (20.19). So, not surprisingly, allusions to the gift of the Spirit appear in the story of Good Friday and

Easter, as if to say, 'Now that the hour and the day are come, the pouring out of Holy Spirit cannot wait.'

In the narrative of Calvary there may be an allusion to the giving of the Spirit when at the moment of the death of Jesus the sentence occurs: 'He gave up his spirit' (19.30). Usually understood to mean that Jesus committed his spirit to the Father in death (cf. Luke 23.46), the sentence may possibly refer in symbol to the giving of the Holy Spirit to the disciples. But there follows an incident whose spiritual symbolism seems to be in no doubt. The soldiers come to break the legs of those who had been crucified so as to hasten their death, but when they come to Jesus they find that he is already dead, and they do not break his legs:

> But one of the soldiers pierced his side with a spear, and at once there came out blood and water. He who saw it has borne witness – his testimony is true, and he knows that he tells the truth – that you also may believe (19.34–5).

Why does the evangelist put such intense emphasis on what may have been a trivial and casual action on the soldier's part? No doubt he is showing his concern for historic fact: Jesus really died, and did not only seem to die. But it is hard to doubt that symbolism is also present. The *water* means cleansing, the *blood* means sacrificial life; and from Christ crucified, cleansing and sacrificial life (each of them linked with one of the sacraments) flow into the lives of those who believe. Water and blood summarize the life in the Spirit; and the pouring out of the gift is now possible because the hour has come and the Christ is glorified.

We pass on to the Easter story, the first day of the week which is also 'that day'. Jesus appears to the eleven. He greets them with his peace, they are glad because they see him, and he shows them his hands and his side. Then:

> Jesus said to them again, 'Peace be with you. As the Father has sent me, even so I send you.' And when he had said this, he breathed on them, and said to them, 'Receive the Holy Spirit. If you forgive the sins of any, they are forgiven; if you retain the sins of any, they are retained' (20.21–3).

Here is the bestowal of Spirit, with the Old Testament imagery of breath. But now it is the breath of Jesus, and the Spirit is indeed the Spirit of Jesus. The breathing suggests a new creation, recalling the account of the first creation in Genesis. As the mission of Jesus was from the Father, so is the apostles' mission from Jesus; and the Spirit is his no less than the Father's.

It seems idle to try to relate historically the breathing of Spirit on Easter Day here described and the Lucan account of the outpouring of Spirit on the day of Pentecost. John is drawing out with vivid symbolism the dependence of the mission of the Paraclete upon the death and the resurrection of Jesus. The theme has been his own, but it is a theme not far from the earliest teaching of the Christian Church.

9

Some Other Writers

We have traced the diversity of thought and language about the Holy Spirit in the apostolic age. Our sources have been the synoptic tradition, the Lucan writings, St Paul and St John's Gospel. The other New Testament writings contain some passages of striking interest, but none which modify our picture of the Christian experience or the trends of Christian theology.

In the Epistle to the Hebrews we have already noticed the passage about Christian initiation which brings out powerfully the role of the Spirit in the anticipation of the age to come (Heb. 6.4–6). We may notice also a reference to apostasy as doing outrage to the Spirit of grace (Heb. 10.29), and a reference to the Spirit in the giving of gifts when the gospel was preached (Heb. 2.4). The statement that Christ offered himself as a sacrifice 'through the eternal Spirit' (Heb. 9.14), perhaps refers not to the Holy Spirit but to the realm of eternal reality in which the author says that Christ's priestly work was done.

In the First Epistle of Peter the salutation at the beginning of the letter has an interesting trinitarian pattern: 'To the exiles of the dispersion ... chosen and destined by God the Father and sanctified by the Spirit for obedience to Jesus Christ and for sprinkling with his blood' (1 Pet. 1.2). In the same chapter the Spirit who inspired the prophets in their foretelling the Messiah is called 'the Spirit of Christ' (1.11). Later in the letter the Spirit who rests upon the Christians in time of persecution is called 'the Spirit of glory and of

God' (4.14). Indeed these references in St Peter's letter give a lovely *speculum* of belief about the Spirit.

The name John belongs by tradition both to the Epistles and to the Apocalypse.

In the First Epistle of John, which has many affinities to the Gospel though it probably has a different author, there is as in the Gospel a sharp feeling of confrontation between the Church and the world. While the writer shows a deep ethical dualism, he avoids the gnostic kind of dualism whose false teaching was disturbing the Church with denials that Jesus Christ 'came in the flesh'. It is in the context of his insistence upon the event of the incarnation that the writer's allusions to the Holy Spirit are made. (He does not call the Spirit by the name Paraclete, and that title is given to 'Jesus Christ the righteous' who is 'an advocate with the Father' (1 John 2.1).

First, we notice that the Spirit gives to the Christians true knowledge about the question of Jesus coming in the flesh. They have been anointed by the Spirit and they 'all know' (2.20). Because of the anointing they do not need to be taught (2.27). No doubt the anointing means the gift of the Spirit in their baptism.

Akin to this teaching is the plea in chapter 4.1–6 that the members of the Church will test the spirits and discriminate between those who confess that Jesus Christ is come in the flesh and those who deny this. It is the contrast between a spirit which is not of God and is of falsehood and a spirit which is of God and of the truth. The writer is here drawing upon a kind of dualistic language which is found in the Dead Sea Scrolls.[1]

Next, we notice two passages about the presence of

the Spirit being proof that Jesus Christ dwells in the Christians.

> All who keep his commandments abide in him, and he in them. And by this we know that he abides in us, by the Spirit which he has given us (1 John 3.24).

> By this we know that we abide in him and he in us, because he has given us of his own Spirit (4.13).

It is not said what are the marks or evidence of the Spirit's presence. Perhaps the readers will know, and perhaps the presence of prophetic utterance is the evidence in view.

Finally, there is the striking passage about the Spirit, the water, and the blood:

> This is he who came by water and blood, Jesus Christ, not with the water only but with the water and the blood. And the Spirit is the witness, because the Spirit is the truth. There are three witnesses, the Spirit, the water, and the blood; and these three agree (5.6–8).

It is hard to doubt that 'the water' is an allusion to the baptism of Jesus and 'the blood' an allusion to his death. Commentators have differed, however, about the further possibility of an allusion to the sacraments of baptism and the Eucharist, and to the episode in John 19.34 where it is recorded that water and blood flowed from the side of Jesus when it had been pierced by the lance.

The coming of Jesus by the water and the blood suggests his baptism in Jordan and his death on Calvary which were the beginning and the ending of his mission. But why does the writer add, 'not with the water only but with the water *and* the blood'? Perhaps it is because there were heretics who denied that Jesus really died. It is the phrase 'not with the water only ...' which makes it probable that the reference is to the baptism and the death rather than to the water and the blood which flowed from the side.

Then follows the reference to the three witnesses, 'the Spirit, the water, and the blood', whose combined evidence attests the truth of the Son of God. The writer may be thinking of the Spirit's presence in both the baptism and the death, for the Spirit descended upon Jesus at his baptism and was given up by Jesus in his death (John 19.30). Or he may be thinking of the scene on Calvary when Jesus gave up his Spirit and water and blood flowed from his side (so E. C. Hoskyns). Or he may be thinking of the two sacraments which are, in the continuing life of the Church, the counterparts of the historical baptism and death of Jesus. There is ground for hesitation about this view, as evidence is lacking that the term 'the blood' was used as a name for the Eucharist.[2] But C. H. Dodd favoured the view that the sacraments are in the writer's mind: 'Thus apostolic faith is authenticated against false teaching by a threefold testimony: the living word of prophecy and the evangelical sacrament and *the three of them are in accord.*'[3]

Whether or not the sacraments are specifically here in mind it is clear that the Spirit's witness is inseparable from the witness of the coming of Jesus and the death of Jesus in the flesh.

In the Apocalypse the author refers to the Spirit with striking poetic vividness:

John to the seven churches that are in Asia: Grace

to you and peace from him who is and who was and who is to come, and from the seven spirits who are before his throne, and from Jesus Christ the faithful witness, the first-born of the dead, and the ruler of kings on earth (Rev. 1.4–5).

The seven spirits correspond to the seven churches to which the message is addressed, and in each case the refrain recurs:

He who has an ear, let him hear what the Spirit says to the churches (Rev. 2.7, etc.).

Who are the seven spirits? It has been suggested that they are angelic beings used as messengers of the risen Lord; and this is indeed congruous with the description of them as 'torches of fire' which blaze before the throne (4.5). But it is more probable that the spirits are a plural description of the one divine Spirit, for they are linked with the Father and with Jesus Christ in the initial blessing, and the message to each of the seven churches ends with a plea to hear what the Spirit says to them. Furthermore, the spirits are called the eyes of the Lamb (5.6). The one divine Spirit has a sevenfold relation to the churches to which he speaks.

Here indeed is the prophetic rule of the Spirit. Each of the seven messages is described as the Spirit speaking and each begins with a sentence attributing the message to the glorified Christ. The Spirit's messages are Christ's messages, and the relationship is summed up later in the words: 'The testimony of Jesus is the spirit of prophecy' (19.10). The Spirit is the source of prophecy in the Church and prophecy is a witnessing to Jesus. This teaching echoes the conception of the role of prophecy in St Paul, as well as the relation between

Christ and the Paraclete in the Fourth Gospel. The invitation in the Gospel, 'If any one thirst, let him come to me and drink' (John 7.37) is echoed in the final invitation in the Apocalypse:

> The Spirit and the Bride say, 'Come'. And let him who hears say, 'Come'. And let him who is thirsty come, let him who desires take the water of life without price (Rev. 22.17).

10
Afterthoughts

We have reached the end of our study of the experience and the theology of the Holy Spirit in the apostolic age. It was an age in which the Christian gospel moved into different cultural settings and found much variety in emphasis and presentation. Amidst the diversity of concept and expression the underlying unity of faith is striking. In each of the phases of tradition and in each of the writers we have examined, there is the constant link between the Holy Spirit and the historical events of the mission of Jesus the Christ. There is the constant belief that as Jesus did the work of God in his mission in history, so the Spirit continues the work of Jesus which is also the work of God. Furthermore, however the *future* role of the Christians is formulated, the Spirit is the dominant factor in that role. In the Pauline Epistles the Spirit is the first-fruits of the heavenly age. In the Lucan writings the Spirit is the guide and inspirer of the Church's continuing life. In St John the Paraclete mediates the return of Christ to the disciples and brings heavenly comfort in the midst of their tribulation. Those facets seem to be complementary to one another. Whether the Christians look to the past, or to the present, or to a continuing future, or to the end of time, the Spirit brings the power of Christ to them. At every stage in the developing teaching of the Church impersonal language about the Spirit appears as a reminder of the background of Hebrew theology, while the emergence of the language of 'he' rather than 'it' – seen in the

Pauline, Lucan, and Petrine, as well as the Johannine, writings – seems a spontaneous realization rather than the pressing of a theory.

This underlying unity suggests caution in the extent to which we speak, as is now fashionable, of the doctrinal 'pluralism' of the New Testament. But if we ask the books of the New Testament to furnish a 'doctrine of the Spirit', we find that the answer is an incomplete one, for while these books answer many questions they also pose some questions for the Church still to answer. Some of the questions came to be answered within the tradition of the Church, some of them call for a continuing answer in the Church's thought and experience.

In these afterthoughts of our study, three themes call for exploration as we try to evaluate the teaching of the New Testament in a wider context. There is the theme of the Holy Spirit and the triune God, the theme of the Holy Spirit and the world, and the theme of the Holy Spirit and renewal. These are continuing themes of Christian exploration and debate. What light does our study throw upon them?

THE SPIRIT AND THE TRIUNE GOD

It was once fashionable to derive the doctrine of the triune God from proof texts like the trinitarian blessing in 2 Corinthians 13.14, or the command to the disciples in Matthew 28.19, to baptize in the threefold name. Few theologians today would follow that procedure. One reason is that critical opinion, even of a very moderate kind, would question the authenticity of the saying in Matthew 28.19 in its present form. But a deeper reason is that theologians have come to think of revelation not as the utterance of propositions about God but as God's self-disclosure through events, the impact of the events upon those who experience them, and the interpretation of those events in the Christian community. Thus it is held that the first Christians began with the monotheism of Israel and, without abandoning that monotheism, were led by the impact of Jesus upon them to worship Jesus as divine, and were aware that divine spirit within them enabled both their access to God as Father and their response to Jesus as Lord. The readers of this book may judge whether our study of the Holy Spirit corroborates this view of divine revelation.

Often we have noticed that the Holy Spirit is described as the Spirit of God and the Spirit of Jesus. Yet to say only that the Spirit is the impact of God or the impact of Jesus is to do less than justice to the Christian experience, for the Holy Spirit was felt to be one who from within the Christians' own lives makes response to Jesus and to the Father. 'Deep answers unto deep. The deep of God above us and around us is inaudible save as it is answered by the deep of God within us.'[1] It is here that the doctrine of the triune God begins to emerge, not only as a mode of the divine activity but as a relationship within the life of deity. In knowing 'the grace of the Lord Jesus Christ and the love of God and the fellowship of the Holy Spirit' (2 Cor. 13.14), and in having access through Jesus 'in one Spirit to the Father' (Eph. 2.18), the Christians were encountering not only their own relation to God but the relation of God to God. When the Spirit cries in us, 'Abba, Father' and prompts us to say, 'Jesus is Lord', there is God within responding to God beyond. The Fourth Gospel takes the further step of suggesting that the divine relationship, known in the historic mission of Jesus and its sequel, reflects the being of God in eternity. Here the key is found in John's concept of the glory. The glory of self-giving love in the passion and the mission of the Paraclete is one with the glory of God before the world began.

Discussing the origins of the doctrine of the Trinity, Maurice Wiles has suggested that, if the idea of revelation through propositions in Scripture has been abandoned, there are two possible ways of understanding the origin and significance of the doctrine of the Trinity. One is the view of Karl Barth that there is an inherent threefoldness in every act of God's self-revelation. The other, which Dr Wiles himself commends, is that trinitarian doctrine is 'an arbitrary analysis of the activity of God which, though of value in Christian thought and devotion, is not of essential significance'.[2]

There is, however, a striking discussion of the Trinity in an earlier Anglican work of the present century, R. C. Moberly's *Atonement and Personality* (1901). Moberly anticipates Barth's concept of an inherent threefoldness in the divine activity and employs an analogy from the nature of man:

There is the man as he really is in himself, invisible and indeed inaccessible – and yet directly the fountain, origin, and cause of everything that can be called in any sense himself. Secondly there is himself as projected into conditions of visibleness – the overt expression or utterance of himself. And thirdly there is the reply of what we call external nature to him – his operation or effect ... In a word there is the echo or image of himself, responsive to himself, which comes back to him from without.[3]

Here indeed is an analysis of an inherent threefoldness in the self-realization of a person which provides an analogy for a like threefoldness in the action of God in relation to the created world. Our study of the Holy Spirit in the apostolic age suggests that God did reveal himself in such threefold manner. In the story which we have been tracing, the invisible God is made known in the visible mission of the Christ and in the response of the Spirit to him from within human lives. Readers of this book may be able to consider whether it is 'arbitrary' or 'not of essential significance' to believe that God so acted and so revealed himself as he eternally is.

THE SPIRIT AND THE WORLD

Throughout our study it has been apparent that, in the apostolic age, the language about the Holy Spirit was concentrated within the orbit of the mission of Jesus and the community of believers who were themselves the beginning of the new creation and the heirs of the world to come. The term Holy Spirit is never used of the activity of God in the wider sphere of the created world, so intense is the concentration upon the new order which the gospel has inaugurated. It is the eschatological note which predominates: Holy Spirit is the power of the age to come, breaking into the last phase of human history.

The first Christians, however, for all the intensity of their experience of the Holy Spirit in the *ecclesia*, had not abandoned the belief that God was the world's creator, active within it, and making himself known to the minds and consciences of men. They would not repudiate the Old Testament teaching about the divine *ruach*, nor the teaching of the Wisdom writers about the operations of the divine wisdom such as the Book of Proverbs or the Book of Wisdom describe. Indeed St Paul, viewing the corrupt society of his time, wrote:

> For what can be known about God is plain to them, because God has shown it to them. Ever since the creation of the world his invisible nature, namely, his eternal power and deity, has been clearly perceived in the things that have been made. So they are without excuse (Rom. 1.19–20).

Akin to this is St Paul's preaching at Athens as St Luke describes it. There he quotes the poet Aratus to illustrate his theme that God created the human race with the power to feel after him and find him (Acts 17.22–9). A few other echoes of this doctrine occur in the apostolic age. But the most thorough and influential expression of the divine activity in the created world comes in the prologue of St John's Gospel:

> In the beginning was the Word, and the Word was with God, and the Word was God. He was in the beginning with God; all things were made through him, and without him was not anything made that was made. In him was life, and the life was the light of men. The light shines in the darkness, and the darkness has not overcome it (John 1.1–5).

These words have come to be the classical statement on their theme. It may here be added that the theme in the Epistle to the Colossians of the gathering-up of all things in Christ as the one in whom the universe is to be united seems to imply a cosmic divine activity of which Christ is the completion.

In the Church of the early centuries it was the tendency to continue the terminology found in the New Testament writings. The Greek and Latin Fathers, when they wrote of the activity of God in nature or in pagan philosophy, would use the term *Logos* rather than Spirit. Such was the concentration of the Church upon the sphere of redemption and often upon hostility to the world, that a Christian concern about the presence of God in nature was often far to seek. Where a Christian joy in nature found expression, as in Clement and Origen in Alexandria and Basil and Gregory of Nyssa in Cappadocia, the word 'Spirit' was not the word they used. St Basil could write, 'I want creation to thrill you with such wonder that everywhere every tiny plant may remind you of its neighbour' (*Discourse* 9.1); and modern theologians have been surprised that the word Spirit does not occur.[4]

If, superficially, it seems that both the New Testament and the early Church encourage a dichotomy of terms, Spirit for God's action in the *ecclesia* and the Word for God's action in the world, it would be a serious mistake to leave the question there. Neither Scripture nor the early Church encourages a departmentalizing of the activity of Father, Son, and Spirit; both emphasize strongly the unity of God. God, Father and Son and Spirit, is at work as creator; God, Father and Son and Spirit, is at work as redeemer. The Old Testament language about the action of *ruach* in the world is not abrogated, nor is the identification of Spirit and Wisdom. As the action of Christ in the Church includes the Spirit's kindling of the believers' responses, so the action of the Word in the world will include the Spirit's kindling of human responses.

The issue therefore is not one of terminology, or of

persons of the triune God. It is the issue of the relation between the action of God in the *ecclesia* as the eschatological community upon which the New Testament doctrine of the Spirit is concentrated, and the action of God in the created world near and far. It is the continuing task of theology to think out as far as possible the relation between these two spheres, and the task is made both more feasible and more necessary by the enhanced knowledge of nature in the modern world.

It is here possible to do no more than to indicate some of the problems, and to ask what light is cast upon them by our study of the Holy Spirit. There is the question of the sciences, the question of the world religions, and the question of diffused goodness in the human race.

As God is the author of all truth and the source of every quest for truth in the human race, the sciences are disclosures of his truth. So truth disclosed in certain of the sciences can illuminate the Christians' understanding of God's revelation of himself in Holy Scripture. Thus the advance of evolutionary biology has enabled a new understanding of the wonder of divine creation as a process through many stages of nature, with man as the climax. So too the advance of historical science and literary criticism has enabled Christians to perceive God's self-revelation in the Bible not only through literalistic statements but through a variety of literary media: drama, poetry, myth, symbol, as well as history. But while the sciences serve God's truth, there can be 'mythologies' in connection with them which disturb truth, such as myths of 'inevitable progress' or 'the scientific mind'. If the sciences illustrate the Johannine concept of the light that lightens every man, they do not reveal or discover what is revealed when the Word became flesh and dwelt among us, nor do they supersede what St Paul called the wisdom of the cross.

The greater involvement of the adherents of the world's religions with one another is bringing to an end the isolationism which used to prevail. The Christian finds himself approaching other religions with reverence and humility. Taught by the Johannine prologue he will know that in the other religions there is truth and goodness derived from the light that lightens every man. At the same time he believes that Jesus is the perfect revelation of God, the fulfilment of all that is true, the final Word. The Christian is likely to witness to this if his concern is less to promote Christianity as a system than to show Christ and to find Christ. The missionary brings Christ to those of other faiths while he is awake to finding Christ there. It is thus that he may help people to acknowledge as Lord and Saviour[5] the Christ who has been among them.

The diffused goodness seen in the human race is often a challenge to the exclusiveness of Christian language about the Holy Spirit. It is asked whether or how the goodness of those who conscientiously respond to the best that they know, differs from the goodness of those who respond in faith to Jesus Christ and invoke the Holy Spirit. Here I mention only one consideration which our study of the Holy Spirit will have suggested. Goodness has God as its author and to belittle any goodness may be to blaspheme the divine Word who is its author. Yet, for the world's salvation, it is the work of the Holy Spirit not only to produce goodness in human lives but to lead human lives to acknowledge God as the author of goodness and to glorify Christ. The life of salvation is the life whose goodness is humbled in the presence of him who is its author and its goal.

So these three issues are raised by the relation of the Spirit in the *ecclesia* and the Spirit in the world: the sciences, the world religions, the diffused goodness in the world. Each of these issues calls for the uninhibited recognition of the divine Word, and therefore Spirit, in the world, and also for the acknowledgement of a divine Saviour without whom neither science, nor religion, nor goodness, can climb to heaven – for heaven is the perfect sharing in the glory of God through the Spirit. The pattern of our answer will still be the pattern of the prologue: that the world was created through the Word, that in him was life and the life was the light of men, and that the Word was made flesh and they saw his glory. But this answer is credible only when it is reflected in the humility, the penitence, the compassion, the integrity of those who belong to Christ. It is thus, and only thus, that the Paraclete takes 'what is mine' and declares it to the disciples.

So we are led inexorably to the theme of renewal.

THE SPIRIT AND RENEWAL

At the present time there is in many parts of Christendom a spiritual liveliness with a belief in the power of the Holy Spirit to renew the Church. Here is a typical expression. In June 1968 the Metropolitan Ignatias of Latakia, addressing the Assembly of the World Council of Churches at Uppsala, said:

Without the Holy Spirit God is far away.
   Christ stays in the past,

   the Gospel is simply an organization,
   authority a matter of propaganda,
   the liturgy is no more than an evolution,
   Christian loving a slave morality.
But in the Holy Spirit
   the cosmos is resurrected and grows
   with the birth pangs of the Kingdom,
   the Risen Christ is there,
   the Gospel is the power of life,
   the Church shows forth the life of the Trinity,
   authority is a liberating science,
   mission is a Pentecost,
   the liturgy is both renewal and anticipation,
   human action is deified.

These words, with a characteristic blending of rhetoric and theological perception, express much of the enthusiasm which has returned. But they are not far from what traditional orthodoxy has often said. Bishop Charles Gore used to say that when he recited in the Creed, 'I believe in the Holy Catholic Church,' he meant: 'I believe in the Holy Spirit revivifying the Church.'

What considerations about renewal does our study of the apostolic age suggest?

There is room for an ecclesiology which gives the Spirit a greater place than much of the familiar ecclesiology in the West has done. In the West a Christological understanding of the Church has prevailed, and it has been possible to concentrate upon the concept of the Body of Christ in such a way as to suggest a rather static and institutionalized doctrine. But while indeed the Church's sacramental and apostolic order witnesses to the historical givenness of gospel and

Church, there is need to remember the continuing lively action of the Spirit whereby alone the believers are Christ's body. The many *charismata* shared among the Church's members are not personal qualities or possessions so much as constant actions of the Spirit in which the liveliness of God touches human lives. In every epoch the Spirit is invading *ruach* as well as indwelling *pneuma*.

But to re-emphasize, the Spirit in the pattern of theology does not of itself lead to spiritual renewal because the assertion of a theology of the Spirit may become a 'thing-in-itself' and what began as liveliness of understanding may pass into being a new conventionalism. It is to minds and hearts and wills which are ever open, ever receptive, that the Spirit speaks, while they on their part test what is of the Spirit by the test of witness to the crucified and risen Jesus.

It is often in groups of Christians meeting for prayer together that a new openness to the Spirit is discovered. It is in such groups that it is vividly realized that the prayer of Christians is not of their own strength or initiative; the Spirit prays within them and they participate in the Spirit's prayer. There can be a rediscovery of what the Epistle to the Ephesians described:

Do not get drunk with wine, for that is debauchery; but be filled with the Spirit, *addressing one another* in psalms and hymns and spiritual songs, singing and making melody to the Lord with all your heart ... (Eph. 5.18–19).

It is in this context that *glossolalia* or speaking with tongues may be significant. This is described as a breach in the reserve which we assume as a system of defence. It helps us to cross the threshold and, in doing so, attain a new freedom in our surrender to God. In psychological terms, we should say that it is the voice of the subconscious rising to God, finding a manner of praying which is analogous to other expressions of our subconscious in dreams, laughter, tears, painting or dance. This prayer within the depths of our being heals, at a profound yet often perceptible level, hidden psychological wounds that impede full development of our interior life.[6]

When spiritual renewal happens, with the revival of *glossolalia* and other gifts, the term 'charismatic revival' is commonly used. Such revival may be powerful within the Church's sacramental life without division or disruption. The danger is any tendency to treat *glossolalia*, or any single gift, as the mark of the normal or the mature Christian, with the implication that Christians without that gift are somehow defective. To do that is to 'institutionalize' a particular experience. But openness to the Spirit comes in many expressions, and among them are the gifts of courageous intellectual integrity and outgoing service to human needs. St Paul's advice to the church of Corinth still stands.

If 'charismatic renewal' is a phenomenon within the life of many churches, 'Pentecostalism' denotes a distinctive doctrine concerning baptism and the Holy Spirit.

Essentially the doctrine is this: after conversion (and water baptism) there remains a *second blessing* in which one receives the fulness of the Holy Spirit, and his personal indwelling, experiencing in oneself what the first disciples experienced at Pentecost.

Some manifestation, usually tongues, is generally expected; indeed strict Pentecostals demand it – 'no tongues, no tongues, no baptism in the Spirit'.[7]

Two questions here arise for us: the one concerns New Testament exegesis, and the other concerns the nature of the spiritual life of a Christian.

It is urged that the Baptist's prediction, 'he shall baptize you with the Holy Spirit' was fulfilled not in the sacramental rite of baptism in water, with the gift of Holy Spirit linked with it, but in occasions – apart from the sacramental rite – when the Spirit was poured out and signs such as *glossolalia* followed. Here let it only be said that the evidence as interpreted by the weight of New Testament scholarship, points to the view that baptism was the sacramental rite given once for all to converts to Jesus as Lord. Subsequent gifts and manifestations of the Spirit in Christian lives are the realization of the meaning and power of the gift which was in baptism once bestowed.

The spiritual life of a Christian is a growing apprehension of what his baptism meant. That growing apprehension may involve varieties of experiences sometimes in gradual growth, sometimes in particular moments of grace. It is a mistake to stereotype one particular moment described as 'the second blessing'. By the power of the Spirit we press on to apprehend that for which we were once for all apprehended. 'Become what you are' is the law of the Christian life. For some this happens in great moments of spiritual awakening, for others in a continuing death-to-self. It is a mistake when dramatic experiences, which can do so much for the renewal of the Church's liveliness, are linked with arbitrary doctrines concerning baptism and second blessing, thereby producing a new divisive institutionalism.

The Spirit's renewal of the Church is linked with the Spirit's witness to the life, death, and resurrection of Jesus. The way of truth along which the Paraclete leads is always the way that is Christ himself, as he takes the things of Christ and declares them to the disciples.

At the present time there are attempts to understand Christian spirituality as an experience somewhat apart from the historical events of the gospel. Our study has shown how in the apostolic age the events and the experience are interwoven. No account of the experience is more vivid than that which St Paul gives in the opening section of Romans 5. The Christians are justified by faith, they have peace with God, they rejoice in hope, and they rejoice even in suffering, because the love of God was poured into their hearts by the Spirit. But what is this love of God? It is the love made known in the death of Christ for the sake of the ungodly, and in that death the love of God himself was commended to men. The event of the death of Christ not only enables the Christian life, it provides its continuing motive and interpretation. 'It is folly', wrote Baron von Hugel, 'to attempt the finding of a shorter way to God than that of the closest contact with his own condescension.'[8]

But it is a costly thing to invoke the Spirit, for the glory of Calvary was the cost of the Spirit's mission and is the cost of the Spirit's renewal. It is in the shadow of the cross that in any age of history Christians pray: Come, thou holy Paraclete.

Notes

CHAPTER 1
HOLY SPIRIT

1 The 'elusiveness' of Spirit, in both Testaments, is well discussed by R. P. C. Hanson in *The Attractiveness of God* (SPCK 1973), ch. 6.
2 Instances are given by Schweizer, *Spirit of God* (Bible Key Words, from G. Kittel's *Theologisches Wörterbuch*) (A. & C. Black 1960), p. 14.
3 See Schweizer, op. cit., pp. 17–18.

CHAPTER 2
THE SPIRIT IN THE MISSION OF JESUS

1 Cf. Rudolf Bultmann, *Theology of the New Testament* (Eng. trans., SCM Press 1952), vol. 1, pp. 153–64.
2 C. K. Barrett, *The Holy Spirit and the Gospel Tradition* (SPCK 1947), p. 39, where the evidence is cited in full.
3 J. G. D. Dunn, *Jesus and the Spirit* (SCM Press 1975), p. 90.
4 Cf. J. Jeremias, *New Testament Theology*, pt. 1 (Eng. trans., SCM Press 1971), pp. 61–7.
5 Dunn, op. cit.
6 Cf. the discussion in C. K. Barrett, op. cit., pp. 140–60.
7 R. N. Flew, *Jesus and His Church* (Epworth Press 1938), p. 71.

CHAPTER 3
ST LUKE: NAZARETH, JERUSALEM, ROME

1 See below, pp. 46–7.
2 On the issues in the birth narrative, see G. B. Caird, *The Gospel of St Luke*, Pelican Gospel Commentaries (Penguin 1971), pp. 52–6.
3 The possibility of a number of comings of Holy Spirit to groups of disciples in different localities is discussed by J. G. D. Dunn, op. cit., pp. 136–46.

CHAPTER 4
THE WITNESS OF ST PAUL

1 Cf. W. D. Davies, *Paul and Rabbinic Judaism* (SPCK 1970), pp. 153–4.
2 Cf. Davies, op. cit., p. 181.
3 The background is discussed by R. M. Wilson in his essay, 'The Spirit in Gnostic Literature', in *Christ and Spirit in the New Testament*, CUP 1973.
4 The relation of Spirit to the risen Christ in 1 Corinthians 15 is well discussed by J. G. D. Dunn in his essay in *Christ and Spirit in the New Testament*.
5 Schweizer, *Spirit of God*, Bible Key Words, p. 83.
6 K. E. Kirk, 'The Origins of the Doctrine of the Trinity', in *Essays on the Trinity and the Incarnation*, ed. A. E. J. Rowlinson, Longmans 1928.
7 L. S. Thornton, *The Incarnate Lord* (Longmans 1928), pp. 317–27.
8 C. F. D. Moule, 'The Holy Spirit in the Scriptures', in *The Church Quarterly* (April 1971), pp. 284–6.

CHAPTER 5
ST PAUL: THE SPIRIT AND THE CHRISTIAN LIFE

1 J. Jeremias, *New Testament Theology*, Eng. trans., pt. 1, p. 64. Cf. the section on pp. 61–8.
2 C. K. Barrett, *The Epistle to the Romans* (A. & C. Black 1957), p. 157.
3 H. B. Swete, *The Holy Spirit in the New Testament* (Macmillan 1909), p. 221.

CHAPTER 6
SPIRIT, FELLOWSHIP, CHURCH

1 This theme is powerfully developed in John V. Taylor's book, *The Go-Between God*, SCM Press 1972.
2 This discussion does not prejudge the question of the authorship of Ephesians. For the view, widely held among scholars today, that St Paul was not the author, see J. L. Houlden, *Paul's Letters from Prison*, Pelican New Testament Commentaries, Penguin 1970. For the possibility of Pauline authorship, see G. B. Caird, Clarendon Commentaries.
3 The first interpretation is followed by most of the English versions; the second by Armitage Robinson in his *The Epistle*

to the Ephesians ad loc.; and the third by W. L. Knox, *St Paul and the Church of the Gentiles* (CUP 1935), pp. 162–5.

4 John S. Ruef, *St Paul's First Letter to Corinth*, Pelican New Testament Commentaries (Penguin 1971), p. 12.

5 For the meaning of *charismata*, see J. G. D. Dunn, *Jesus and the Spirit*, pp. 199–251.

6 See the valuable discussion of this passage in John S. Ruef's *St Paul's First Letter to Corinth*, ad loc.

CHAPTER 7
ST JOHN: SPIRIT AND GLORY

1 Rudolf Bultmann, *The Gospel of St John: A Commentary* (Eng. trans., Blackwell 1971), p. 9.

2 I have followed here the more intelligible punctuation, adopted in the R.S.V. margin and used by some commentators.

CHAPTER 8
ST JOHN: THE PARACLETE

1 F. J. A. Hort, *The Way, the Truth, the Life*, Hulsean Lectures for 1871, p. 14.

2 For a discussion of the background, see George Johnston, *The Spirit-paraclete in the Gospel of John*, CUP 1970.

3 The problem of language and interpretation of this passage is well discussed by C. K. Barrett, in *The Gospel According to St John* (SPCK 1955), ad loc.

CHAPTER 9
SOME OTHER WRITERS

1 Cf. J. L. Houlden, *Commentary on the Johannine Epistles* (A. & C. Black 1974), pp. 32–3.

2 Cf. Houlden, op. cit., ad loc.

3 Cf. C. H. Dodd, *The Johannine Epistles* (Hodder & Stoughton 1946), pp. 127–31.

CHAPTER 10
AFTERTHOUGHTS

1 W. P. du Bose, *The Gospel in the Gospels* (Longmans 1906), pp. 242–6. I am glad to recall gratefully this creative theological thinker and teacher in the American Episcopal Church.

2 M. F. Wiles, *Working Papers in Christian Doctrine*, pp. 14–15.

3 R. C. Moberly, *Atonement and Personality* (Murray 1901), pp. 173–4. The passage contains illuminating instances of the analogy here described.

4 For these issues in the early Church, see especially C. E. Raven, *Natural Religion and Christian Theology* (CUP 1953), ch. 2: 'Nature in the Early Church'.

5 The questions about Christianity and other religions are discussed with special discernment by Lesslie Newbigin in *The Finality of Christ*, SCM Press 1969.

6 Cardinal Suenens, *A New Pentecost?* (Darton, Longman & Todd 1975), pp. 102–3.

7 Simon Tugwell, O.P., *Did You Receive the Spirit?* (Darton, Longman & Todd 1972), p. 40. This book is marked by sympathy with 'charismatic' Christianity together with shrewd critical judgement.

8 Quoted by E. J. Tinsley in his essay, 'History, Criticism, and Spirituality', in *Christian Spirituality Today*, ed. A. M. Ramsey, Faith Press 1961.

Index of Biblical References

GENESIS	1.2	24, 34
EXODUS	19.6	62
JUDGES	14.6	11
1 SAMUEL	10.10	11
1 KINGS	17.22	11
PSALMS	104.29–32	11
PROVERBS	1.23	11
ISAIAH	11.1–3	14
	61.1–2	14,36
EZEKIEL	11.19–20	12
	36.24–7	13
	37.4–6	13
JOEL	2.28–9	14, 39
MICAH	3.8	12
WISDOM	1.7	17
	6—7	17
MATTHEW	3.7–17	21–2
	10.20	31

MATTHEW (*cont.*)	10.28	28
	12.31–2	29
MARK	1.9–11	23
	3.28–30	29
	13.11	31
LUKE	1.35	34
	3.7–12	21–2
	10.21	28
	11.13	28
	12.10	28
	12.12	31
	12.49–50	22–3
	24.49	31
JOHN	1.1–5	122
	1.32–4	91
	3.1–15	92–3
	4.1–24	93–5
	6.61–3	96
	7.37–9	97, 116
	14—16	100–8
	19.34–5	109
	20.21–3	110
ACTS	2	37–41, 74
	4.31	37
	6—28	40–3
	10.46	43, 81
	17.22–9	122
	19.6	43, 81
ROMANS	1.3–4	53
	5.1–11	55, 131

ROMANS (*cont.*)	8.14–15	66
	8.18–27	71–2
	15.17–19	46, 64
1 CORINTHIANS	1.2	65, 80
	2.4	46, 49
	2.14–16	50
	6.11	64
	12—14	81–4
	12.12	77
	15.44	49
	15.52–3	55
2 CORINTHIANS	3.17–18	55, 60
	13.14	54, 75
GALATIANS	5.4–6	66
	5.16–26	69
EPHESIANS	1.22–3	77
	2.18	55
	2.20–2	64, 77, 79
	4.1–12	78–9
	5.18–19	128
PHILIPPIANS	2.1–7	75–6
COLOSSIANS	3.1–4	58
1 THESSALONIANS	1.4–6	45
	5.23	67–8
HEBREWS	6.4–5	58; 111
	9.14	111
	10.29	64, 111

1 PETER	1.2	111
	2.4–5	79
	2.9	65, 80
1 JOHN	2.20–7	112
	5.6–8	113–14
REVELATION	1.4–5	115
	2.7	115
	19.10	115
	22.17	116